MERCY IN PADRE PIO

STEFANO CAMPANELLA

MERCY IN PADRE PIO

TRANSLATED BY
EDMUND C. LANE, SSP AND ARTHUR PALISADA, SSP

PREFACE BY
RINO FISICHELLA

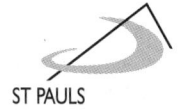

ST PAULS

Library of Congress Cataloging-in-Publication Data
First published in Italy under the title *La Misericordia in Padre Pio* by Edizioni San Paolo s.r.l.

© 2016 Edizioni San Paolo s.r.l.
www.edizionisanpaolo.it; Distribuzione: Diffusione San Paolo s.r.l.
Piazza Soncino, 5 - 20092 Cinisello Balsamo (Milano)

English language edition © 2017 by the Society of St. Paul
English translation by Edmund C. Lane, S.S.P. and Arthur Palisada, S.S.P.

ISBN 978-0-8189-1393-8

Produced and designed in the United States of America
by the Fathers and Brothers of the Society of St. Paul,
2187 Victory Boulevard, Staten Island, New York 10314
as part of their communications apostolate.

ISBN 978-0-8189-1393-8

Printing Information:

Current Printing - first digit	1	2	3	4	5	6	7	8	9	1 0

Year of Current Printing – first year shown

2017	2018	2019	2020	2021	2022	2023	2024	2025	2026	2027

TABLE OF CONTENTS

CHAPTER III
MERCIFUL PADRE PIO

CHAPTER IV
THE "SOCIAL" MERCY OF PADRE PIO

PREFACE

December 8, 2015, with the solemn opening of the Holy Door in St. Peter's Basilica, the Extraordinary Jubilee Year of Mercy, willed by Pope Francis so that all of the Church might direct its glance, in a special way, to the mercy of God begun. This Holy Year, with respect to those preceding it, possessed several new characteristics that Pope Francis enumerated in the Bull of Indiction, *Misericordiae vultus*. Among these, it is worth noting, was the institution of the Missionaries of Mercy. They were some 1000 priests and religious from all over the world, upon whom the Pope personally conferred the mandate to be "a sign of the maternal solicitude of the Church for the People of God, in order that they might enter deeply into the richness of this mystery which is so fundamental to the faith" (MV 18). The Missionaries, invited by the Bishops, went into the dioceses to animate the missions to the people and all those initiatives which have a particular reference to Mercy. They were called especially to undertake their mandate by preaching and hearing confessions. For this reason, Pope Francis granted them the authority to absolve even those sins reserved to the Holy See.

The commissioning of the Missionaries of Mercy took place during a solemn celebration in St. Peter's Basilica on Ash Wednesday. Pope Francis wanted their commissioning to take place in the presence of the relics of St. Padre Pio, together with those of St. Leopoldo Mandic. With this gesture the Pope intended to offer to all priests an example to follow. A huge part of the ministry of Padre Pio and St. Leopoldo, in fact, took place in administering the Sacrament of Reconciliation. Padre Leopoldo is less well known than his confrere in San Giovanni Rotondo, even though both shared in a complementary way the great gift of offering mercy, especially in enabling the penitent to feel the love of God who forgives. We know that Padre Pio spent entire days in the confessional and many were the individuals who each day, from Italy and from all parts of the world, went to him to receive absolution and to hear from him a word of encouragement or some advice. The many testimonials in this regard, some of which have been collected in the beautiful pages of this book, show Padre Pio as a sincere confessor, exigent and at times even severe. From all of them, however, it becomes apparent that each confession profoundly transformed the penitent in such a way as to enable him or her to be reborn to a new Gospel-based life because they had received the forgiveness of God.

The mercy of St. Padre Pio did not end in the confessional. It was also translated into other concrete gestures which enabled him, even in his own body, to experience the love of the Lord. For everyone the construction of the hospital, "Casa Sollievo della Sofferenza," strongly willed and realized by the humble Capuchin who lived in San Giovanni Rotondo, remains an eloquent witness. This excellent structure reminds us that mercy is transformed and made visible even in the aid and support of those who live in difficult situations. Finally, it becomes evident that our faith is made concrete where Jesus is not most of all a doctrine to teach, but a person to meet and a face to contemplate.

These pages offer a portrait of Padre Pio in reference to mercy, trying to tie its various aspects with the living voice of those who, through his work, have experienced it in person. My wish is that reading them may serve as an instrument for living better, following the example of St. Pio of Pietrelcina.

✠ *Rino Fisichella*
President of the Pontifical Council
for the Promotion of the New Evangelization

Chapter 1

PADRE PIO DISPENSER
OF DIVINE MERCY

Padre Pio dedicated a great deal of time to hearing confessions, mainly because there were so many persons who would kneel at his feet in order to obtain absolution. "I don't have a free moment: all my time is spent in absolving my brothers from the bonds of Satan,"[1] he wrote on June 3, 1919, around a month following the first appearance in the news of his stigmata.[2] And he added: "The greatest charity is to snatch souls entwined by Satan to win them over to Christ."[3]

We can easily surmise that this enemy of God and men was well aware of the great pastoral activity that the humble religious from Pietrelcina would have undertaken by means of this specific ministry, seeing that he ended up almost reducing him at the end of his life to being unable to exercise it.

A Ministry Blocked

He had just turned 18 and was attending a course in philosophy;[4] in fact, when Fra Pio became ill with a sickness characterized by weakness and stomach problms,[5] "by fever and severe pain"[6], doctors recommended a bit of native air.[7] The first clinical evaluation, a trace of which has been found, reads, "A weakening of respiratory functioning at the base of the right lung along with an intermittent weakening at the apex of the left lung. Dry cough and challenging night sweats with a persistent but negligible fever." All these symptoms most "probably" refer to "bronchial alveolus in its initial stage."[8] For this reason, at the beginning of October 1907, all of his classmates took their exams in San Marco Catola "in order to pass their course in philosophy and be admitted to the study of theology."[9] All, that is, but him.[10]

Nonetheless Fra Pio was admitted to the first year of theology and moved to the convent of Serracapriola, returning to his family of origin during the summer of 1908 "and again toward the end of the successive school year, which he began in the convent of Montefuso without finishing. His teacher and confessor, Padre Agostino da San Marco in Lamis,[12] to avoid having to postpone the conferring of the order of the diaconate, tried to get his student "dispensed from taking the exams" or to take them "in a simpler way."[13] However it was not possible either to obtain a dispensation from the exams or to obtain a dispensation from the examination through the proposed creation of a "delegation" of examiners composed of the same Padre Agostino and a priest of the Archdiocese of Benevento,[14] because the archbishop, Monsignor Benedetto Bonazzi[15], wanted to examine him personally as soon as his

health condition would permit.[16] Fra Pio started studying. He
had to skip the ordination foreseen for the month of June[17]
and, after having reentered the convent of Morcone,[18] was
ordained deacon on July 28, 1909 in the church annex by
Monsignor Benedetto Della Camera, bishop of Thermopylae[19].
However, even here there was only one month remaining
because his illness had become acute. As a consequence he
was not even able to take the exams in dogmatic theology,
hermeneutics, patrology and Church history which were given
from the 10th to the 12th of October.[20]

At the end of the month his condition had probably im-
proved for Fra Pio began a trip to the convent of Gesualdo,
seat for the study of moral theology, where he may have spent
a couple of months.[21] At the beginning of January 1910, in
fact, he had returned to Pietrelcina. Here a letter from his
Provincial Administrator, Padre Benedetto da San Marco in
Lamis[22], had reached him who had written in resignation:

> "My dearest Fra Pio, if you have experienced a noticeable improve-
> ment in your health as a result of your being able to breathe in your
> native air, continue to stay there, praying that the good God will
> at least make it possible for you to study and to do what is neces-
> sary for your promotion to the priesthood according to the latest
> instructions. What God's purposes are in willing this necessity on
> our family I am unaware; but I embrace them all the same, hoping
> with the utmost confidence that the crisis will be resolved."[23]

The young friar replied asking Padre Benedetto to ask the
Holy See for a dispensation to anticipate his ordination by a few
months with respect to the canonical age,[24] setting forth the
fact that the state of his health was such that the Lord might

soon abbreviate his "exile on earth," and that he would be
"most grateful" because he had no other desire than to become
a priest.[25] Now, in fact, "the idea of a cure" appeared to him like
"a dream, even a word without any sense," while he felt his final
passage "to be very close."[26]

In the meantime he was studying moral theology[27] with
some help some from a local priest, Don Giuseppe Maria
Orlando, who had become his confessor during his stay at
Pietrelcina.[28] Every good proposal was, however, subordinated
to the unstable condition of his health, described in a letter
to his spiritual director, Padre Benedetto da San Marco in
Lamis:

> "My stomach, thank goodness, almost since Christmas no longer
> rejects anything, whereas at the beginning it could not retain
> anything other than plain water. Also I am beginning to regain
> my strength such that I can walk a little without becoming too
> tired. But the thing that doesn't want to leave me is the fever which,
> almost every day toward evening, revisits me followed by copious
> sweats. The cough and chest pains come back and are the things
> which plague me almost constantly."[29]

Perhaps it was the continuous suffering, perhaps the feeling of being close to death already, perhaps waiting for a dispensation which never arrived or perhaps all of these things
taken together ended up by throwing into disarray the spirit
of Fra Pio to the point of making him "cast to the winds" his
hopes and to make him think that he had hoped "uselessly,"
and to want to give up that which constituted a part of his
"consolation." All the same he was ready to accept "the will
of God"[30] and ended up by writing:

"In silence I adore and kiss the hand of the one who is persecuting me, knowing moreover that he is the one who on one hand makes me anxious and on the other hand consoles me."[31]

To complicate the situation further temptations to scruples of conscience were added. He thought that he had often "badly" spent his life, was assaulted by the "thought of not being certain whether or not he had confessed all the sins of […] his past life," and was tormented by the doubt of never having "confessed himself well."[32] Sometimes he had the impression that Jesus was hiding from his soul.[33]

Through these dense black clouds, in early July, a beam of light filtered. He received a letter from Padre Benedetto that communicated: "I've received the dispensation from the canonical age."[34]

The document from the Sacred Congregation of Religious allowed him to anticipate the age of ordination by nine months.[35] He thought in order not to lose any more time to schedule the event from the 10th to the 12th of August. Not earlier because he would take the risk of not being able to complete the necessary preliminary formalities. In the same letter the Provincial exhorted the young friar to return to the cloister in the nearby convent, that of Morcone, to prepare for his ordination "by learning the ceremonies."[36]

Fra Pio obeyed. But not even this attempt had a good outcome. After a day of staying in the place designated, the same evening he was forced to take pen and paper in hand to communicate to Padre Benedetto:

"Dear Padre Provincial,
Yesterday, in obedience, I arrived at Morcone together with Padre

Eugenio, who came to substitute me in Pietrelcina. I must however tell you frankly that, after a day in Morcone, I immediately felt much worse; so much so is this true that in this moment in which I am writing I find myself back in bed on account of weakness caused by the vomiting which has returned."[37]

Padre Tommaso of Monte Sant'Angelo, novice master and convent vicar, not waiting for the letter of Fra Pio to reach its destination and the arrival of a response took the responsibility to give him permission to leave immediately for Pietrelcina, after adding at the bottom of the letter to be sent to Padre Benedetto his note:

"Most reverend Padre, poor Fra Pio, in bed with a fever of 39½° Celsius (103° Fahrenheit) and throwing up everything, decided to leave and has already gone back home; in order not to make his situation worse, out of compassion and supposing that this would be your intention, I gave him permission to go."[38]

The problem of the ceremony remained. Our Friar thought of "asking the pastor of […] the place for help, who spontaneously offered it."[39]

Padre Benedetto once again bowed his head before the will of God and wrote to Fra Pio:

"I'm sorry for you, but I respect the eminent decree by God which, out of his ineffable mercy, would not allow you to remain in that cloister from which he himself with such condescension has called you."[40]

He had no objection to the idea of entrusting to the parish priest of Pietrelcina the task of providing the necessary lessons for our future priest, even entrusting him also to get "in touch with the Archdiocesan Curia," to establish a day for the exams.[41]

The pastor, Padre Salvatore Maria Pannullo, wished the best for the young man whom he had met some nine years earlier.[42] He immediately appreciated his human and spiritual qualities and had followed him and encouraged his vocation. For the friar he was like one of the family and he continued to call him "Uncle Tore," as he did when he was a youngster.

Padre Salvatore was not content with teaching him the necessary liturgical ceremonies for priestly ordination but he did his utmost to solve any other problem that arose. He personally went to Benevento on July 29 to meet with the vicar general, Monsignor Giuseppe Loiacono, and set the date for the exams of his former altar boy.[43] And, having received an opening for the following day, he came back on July 30 to accompany and to proudly assist Fra Pio during the interrogation.

The verdict of the Archdiocesan commission was favorable.[44]

The last obstacle had been overcome.

On August 10th in the choir chapel of the canons of the Cathedral of Benevento, Fra Pio was ordained a priest by Archbishop Paolo Schinosi[45], titular archbishop of Marcianopoli, "Archdeacon and Visitor General of the holy metropolitan Church of Benevento."[46]

At that time, in fact, the archbishop of Benevento, Archbishop Benedetto Bonazzi, was "outside the diocese, in Cava dei Tirreni,"[47] where he had been abbot for eight years.[48] The Vicar, though, had written and had obtained from him the faculty, i.e. the act that allowed the ordination by a bishop different from the ordinary of the place, when he was prevented to do it.[49]

By ordination, Padre Pio also received the right to hear confessions, but he could not exercise it because Padre Benedetto had not authorized him to do so. The newly ordained Capuchin priest repeatedly asked permission, but in vain. In April of 1911 he also did so "on behalf of the parish priest" of Pietrelcina, at least to be able to confess the men only during the period of the Easter duty, explaining, among other things, that the parish priest, taking for granted the permission of the Provincial, had "already informed the people."[50] Padre Benedetto, however, remained adamant, fearing that this ministry could be "greatly harmful to his physical health and possibly even the peace of his soul,"[51] and he was not sure of the young priest's "scientific skills in moral theology"[52] because, as is clear from the above date, he had not followed a regular course of study in the religious houses of the Province and had never participated in "the solution of the moral cases that were discussed every month in the convents of the monastic Province."[53]

There were two preliminary judgments caused by the mysterious illness that had kept him outside the cloister walls. The disease seemed to want to foreclose even the goal of priesthood and subsequently was limiting his ministry. A disease that Padre Benedetto had judged in the first instance was a result of the "divine plan," of an "eminent decree of God," as something "especially permitted by God,"[54] as an expression of the "clear, but mysterious will of God."[55]

But, after years, verifying that the "native air experience had been tried and we saw that it maintains but does not heal,"[56] he began not to believe "that it is the Lord" who wanted Padre Pio "outside the cloister," wondering "why God willed for his greater perfection, to take a soul from the cloister to put him forever in the middle of the secular world"[57] and he came to be convinced that the divine did not in fact[58] have anything to do with that which in fact was a "temptation,"[59] "a diabolical illusion" or "a deception of the enemy."[60]

Only when the Provincial Minister was sure that "grace" was active in the friar of Pietrelcina did he grant the hoped for faculty to hear confessions.

"Divine mercy,"[61] the test passed, defeated the evil plan that would hinder the mission of reconciliation between God and men, of the man who would become, for penitents, "a living image of Christ suffering and risen,"[62] knowing full well that it would be precisely "his ministry as a confessor that would constitute the greatest title of glory and distinctive feature"[63] of that young Capuchin priest.

Satan succeeded once again in keeping Padre Pio out of the confessional in 1931 when a series of lies, apparently reliable, induced the Holy Office to deprive him of "all the powers of the [priestly] ministry, with the exception only of the faculty to celebrate the Holy Mass, but only within the walls of the convent, in the inner shrine, privately, but not in the public church."[64] This time, however, the diabolical plan had no lasting effect over time. On July 14, 1933 the segregated Capuchin was again allowed to celebrate in the convent church and "to hear the sacramental confessions of members of his Religious Order in the same monastery, but outside the Church."[65] Eight months later he was able to return to hearing the confessions of lay men[66] and, after a further two months, also women.[67]

Confessions Become Conversions

One can well understand why the devil tried every means to keep Padre Pio away from the confessional. For his penitents, in fact, the efficacy of the sacrament translated into a real change of life, as is demonstrated by some episodes of which traces still remain among the countless spiritual rebirth stories lived in the shadow of the convent of the Capuchin friars of San Giovanni Rotondo.

Under the seal of confession he brought about the conversion of the lawyer Cesare Festa Genovese, who "had reached one of the most prominent positions" in Freemasonry and led the task "of fighting the Church from the political point of view." Intrigued by the stories that his cousin, Giorgio Festa who was a doctor, told about Padre Pio, in 1921 the lawyer went to San Giovanni Rotondo where the stigmatized Capuchin revealed to him his belonging to the sect. Then "he took him by the hand, stared long into his eyes with a look of infinite pity and tenderness, [...] and began to tell him the parable of the Prodigal Son." So Cesare Festa "after having known neither Church nor sacraments nor prayer for more than twenty-five years, always fed by ideas contrary to the Faith, moved and happy, bowed before the great majesty of that Truth which is the joy and consolation of strong spirits; so that, in the confession of his errors, he chose to impose upon himself a complete renunciation of the false ideals he had hitherto pursued."[68]

He had already left the Masons, but had not yet found faith; instead he found Alberto Del Fante, a merchant of Bologna, who had a degree "in administrative law" awarded by "the University of Voltaire in Paris."[69] After publishing in *Italia Laica* "some articles" against Padre Pio, describing him as "a fraud, a wily individual who could dupe credulous people with his captivating enthusiasm," "the undisputed and indisputable sudden healing of his nephew made him think and reflect." He could not give an explanation of the fact that "science had sentenced him relentlessly" as incurable, and then, suddenly, "he is back healthy, lively, and cheerful as before" and, in addition, "on the exact date, predicted a few days before" by the friar. Del Fante decided to meet him and, in 1930, he went to San Giovanni Rotondo laden with questions.[70] The very evening of his arrival he confessed to Padre Pio, who knew everything about him. He was aware that he had been part of "a society that recognizes God, but which does not love his ministers." And he even knew some of the merchant's behavior "that he could not have known." Despite his skepticism, in that confession Del Fante asked the friar to give him "peace of mind," to give him "some light." Padre Pio promised him, "You will have it if you persist in loving God." At this point the penitent vented saying, "God, God … Why does He not enlighten me, Padre? Why does He not make me believe, why doesn't He want me to become a good Christian?" At that time he did not get a clear answer. But his doubts provided the beginning of a journey that led him to faith, brought about through the astounding healing of his nephew.[71]

The Honorable Giuseppe Caradonna, "a member of the Government and vice-president of the Chamber" during the Fascist period was a "thirty-third degree Freemason."[72] In 1928 he was healed instantly from Addison's disease in San Giovanni Rotondo, where he had gone to please his wife, Michela Giuseppina Tamborino, a fervent woman of faith and a Catholic Action leader. Padre Pio placed his hands on the face of the authoritative Fascist leader. He only said: "We hope in God." And "from Caradonna's face all the blemishes immediately disappeared." But he was not yet converted to the Catholic faith.[73] Another miracle was needed: in April 1945 Padre Pio appeared between him and the firing squad of the partisans who were going to shoot him; "the weapons were prevented from being fired."

This episode did break down any of Caradonna's resistance, who went back to San Giovanni Rotondo and, after having confessed, returned to approach the Eucharistic table[74]. The most sensational conversion, of which many newspapers were occupied in the spring of 1950, was that of the Communist Italia Betti, a math and physics teacher in the high school "Galvani" in Bologna, "a relative of the mayor" of the city, "the honorable Dozza (her brother's wife is the sister of the mayor), the sister of the councilor who celebrated the almost clandestine marriage of Terracini," known throughout the Emilia Romagna because "she acted passionately in bringing new members into the party." They discovered that she had cancer. Her younger sister, Emerita, the only one who had "inherited" the faith of their mother, after much insisting, convinced her to go to San Giovanni Rotondo. "In front of the Capuchin friar, to whom are attributed so many prodigies, Professor Betti felt strangely bewildered; she confided to her sister who was close by that she felt as if she were being pushed toward the altar where Padre Pio was celebrating Mass. Even after the function was over Professor Betti did not want to abandon her sacred place. Only after the insistence of a friar did she decide to leave, but only after having made an appointment for confession the next day [...]. The next day, driven by impulse and emotion, Miss Betti, without waiting her turn, rushed to the confessional and publicly recanted her materialistic ideas and her past."[75]

There was less outcry over the radical change in the life of Giovanni Bardazzi, a taxi driver from Prato who spent more time in the "House of the People, the seat of the Communist Party," than in his own home and only set foot in church "once a year, to satisfy his wife but whose ideas were completely opposite to hers."[76] He was "also in Moscow, in 1947, with Togliatti."[77] Padre Pio, through bilocation, went to see him in his bedroom at night and said, "Enough now! I will see you in S. Giovanni Rotondo."[78] This was the mainspring that triggered in him the desire to know this Capuchin about whom his very Catholic wife, who always prayed for his conversion, continually spoke. During the trip, Giovanni said to himself, "Now I am going to this friar and explain to him what is happening, about party matters of which he couldn't possibly know anything. What could you expect a friar to know? And when I have explained it all to him his jaw will drop, he will say that I am right and he too will become communist."[79] Having arrived at the place there were other supernatural signs, and as a result he had to leave without receiving absolution and without having been able to explain his reasons to Padre Pio, who closed the door of the confessional in his face.[80] On two other occasions Bardazzi did not receive absolution from the friar, who granted it only after he saw in him a real change of mentality, followed by an even more rapid change of lifestyle.[81]

Surly Only in Appearance

There are many people who have had the same traumatic experience of Giovanni Bardazzi. But some not only got up from kneeling without absolution, but also had to suffer the

humiliation of being thrown out with a loud voice in front of
other penitents waiting their turn. Fra Eusebio Notte, who for
five years had been the defender of the aged and revered son
of Saint Francis, writes:

> "The confessional was the only way to approach Padre Pio and ask
> him for some advice; so everyone wanted to go to confession to
> him. A huge crowd would gather, with their own way of behaving
> … consisting of quarrels, brawls, bad language, etc. … in order to
> achieve their purpose. No one thought about the accusation of sin
> and repentance. This is one of the main reasons why the Padre sent
> them away without absolution. He did not want to be involved in
> the profanation of the sacrament of confession!
>
> It was then that the Superior had the idea of having people make
> an appointment: a really strange thing, but in a sense it solved
> the problem.
>
> Fifty or sixty women, who presumably confessed to the Padre every
> morning, were prepared in the way they should confess.
>
> Do not start with questions or requests for material things: these
> were reserved to the end of the confession. Priority was given to
> mortal sins, the number, species, etc. and then to venial sins.
>
> To obtain absolution from Padre Pio and the forgiveness of God
> for these sins, an important matter was presumed: to acknowledge
> having sinned, transgressing the commandments of the Lord, and
> to repent […]. Then absolution was guaranteed and they would
> find in Padre Pio not a judge, but a Padre with infinite tenderness,
> inviting you to conversion and a change of life.
>
> A confession made in this way authorized them to ask the Padre
> anything they desired.
>
> If you do not follow these rules, or worse, if there was no certain
> repentance, it would cause the Padre to close the door in his or her

face without much grace. [...] It should be noted, however, that he did not send you to hell, but would always add: "Go away and come back in a month, two months," etc. Return and conversion were almost certain, sealed by a sweet and memorable confession."[82]

Padre Pio himself testified, in his own hand:

"All this can be summed up in this: that they be consumed by love of God and love of neighbor. God for me is always fixed in my mind and imprinted in my heart. I never lose sight of him: I am drawn to admire his beauty, his smiles, and his troubles, his mercies, his revenge or better the rigors of his justice [...]. Believe me, Padre, the outbursts that I am sometimes guilty of, are caused by the thought of his harsh punishment [...]. How can you see God who grieves over evil and not grieve equally? How can you see God who is about to hurl his thunderbolts, and not ward them off by raising a hand to hold his arm if there is no other remedy, and the other is to turn excitedly on your own brother for two reasons: to cast out the evil and that which accosts him, and soon, from the place where they are, because the hand of the judge is about to unload on him? Believe me, though, at this time I am not shaken or in the least bit changed. I do not feel anything but to have and to want what God wants. And in him I feel always at ease, at least always within myself; externally I am sometimes a bit uncomfortable."[83]

When, then, the need for a pedagogical reproach was no longer needed, the face of the stigmatized Capuchin became immediately serene. Padre Carmelo Durante Sessano del Molise, who was the Guardian of the convent of San Giovanni Rotondo from 1953 to 1959, related two eloquent memories:

"After a reprimand, it was enough for him to turn his head to see him smiling again as if nothing had happened. I happened to observe it once and I was surprised, so much so that I said: 'But, Padre, awhile ago it seemed that the world was about to end, but now everything is heaven!' He said, 'My son, I am troubled only on the surface; but inside, in my heart, there is always great calm and serenity.'"[84]

"One day he treated a soul badly. At the complaint of a person who was present: 'But, Padre, you have killed his soul!' He explained: 'No, I have caused anguish to his heart!'"[85]

For a special Minister of Reconciliation there was, therefore, a special requirement. He, in fact, "warned priests not to mock it. To a confessor who sent away a penitent who never returned, he said: 'This is a luxury that you can not afford...'"[86] On another occasion, when some fellow priests asked him, "When you do not absolve, those souls come to us. How are we to act: absolve or not?" He replied: "You must absolve. Padre Pio is just one man."[87] Direct contacts with the Lord, in fact, allowed that friar not only to peer into hearts, but also to know the most effective process of purification to obtain from sinners a deeper repentance, a real renewal.

To one of his brothers he would explain his behavior: "If I see that there is no repentance, I cannot give absolution."[88]

Once Padre Pellegrino Funicelli, who enjoyed an easy familiarity with him, asked: "Those women who left without absolution, in case of sudden death, do they run the risk of being damned?" The saint replied, "But who can say that those souls are in God's disfavor?" Padre Pellegrino objected: "If they are not out of favor with God, why can't they approach the Eucharist?" He replied: "Because they have to perform a particular penance."

In some cases it was he himself who advised those whom he had not forgiven, "Go to someone else for confession."[89]

That way of acting was, however, so out of the ordinary that even the Pope, Pius XII, was told about it. Receiving in audience a group of pilgrims from Tuscany who were staying in Rome as they returned from Gargano, the Pope heard shouting: "Your Holiness, we have come from San Giovanni Rotondo." The Holy Father approached them and asked for news about Padre Pio. "We went to confession to him," they answered, "but none of us received absolution." "They tell me," Pope Pacelli replied, "that the holy man often denies absolution." And then he said, "Do those who have not received absolution go back later?" "Most," the Tuscan pilgrims admitted. "Then," the Pope concluded, "When you go back, tell him on my behalf that he should keep doing the same."[90]

Severity and Fatherly Love

"In the ministry of the confessional Padre Pio sought only the salvation of souls."[91] "He conceived his role as confessor as an aid to the rebirth of people, in making them new. It was in the confessional that he was an educator according to the etymological meaning of this term, which refers to one's ability to bring out in a person his or her true self, beyond all obstacles and limitations. And his harshness was a manifestation of his awareness, for his part, than this was a delicate task!"[92] In fact, he warned: "We priests administer the blood of Christ. We must be careful not to treat it lightly and casually."[93] And, when a priest tried to plead the cause of a penitent sent away without absolution, the holy Capuchin said, "Even you do not understand me? If you knew how I suffer in having to refuse absolution! … Don't you know that it is better to be rebuked by a man on this earth than by God in the Hereafter."[94]

Padre Pio, therefore, did not want to "humiliate the sinner, making him or her feel the weight of their misery," but "to make them face and assume the responsibility that the salvation offered to them provided."[95] "His mission was truly and deeply pedagogical"[96] and had the objective to make the sinner "understand that after the confession he belongs to a new life, in which it was necessary to live and act according to the beautiful, holy plan of God that God had meant for us."[97] That's why, next to those who remember Padre Pio as being "gruff," there are also many who experienced him as a loving father, sensitive and merciful. These are the ones who knelt before him truly repentant and with the firm intention of abandoning the path of sin.

This is demonstrated by the testimony of a nun, his penitent:

> "He was a stern judge when it was necessary to be so (I've often experienced this personally), but then the soul immediately felt the tender Padre who came to shed tears of compassion and love for it."[98]

Even more significant in this regard is an episode of which Professor Francesco Lotti, former head of Pediatrics of the "Casa Sollievo della Sofferenza," was the indirect protagonist as was narrated several times by the same doctor.

> "One day I was waiting to go to confession. An individual from here[99] approached me. He was very upset and told me: "Look. Do you know me?"

"Yes, of course I know you."

"You know, I want you to do me a favor…."

"If I can. Tell me what it is."

"You should tell Padre Pio that if I go to confession to him, that he not treat me badly."

"But, I don't understand. Padre Pio doesn't treat people badly…"

"No. Hear, this is what happened to me; unfortunately I had an affair with a girl, and now it seems that she is expecting a baby. And I, therefore, in my position … if this scandal were to become known…"

Back then it was not like it is today. Today these things no longer make much of an impression. Then things were certainly very important.

He tells me: "I want to go to confession to him, but I don't dare, if he could hear me apart from everyone … you understand … in my position…."

"Well," I say, "I do not know … I'll see if I can say something to Padre Pio … Let's see."

After my confession I say: "Padre, don't you see …"

"What do I not see?"

"Eh, it is this, you know, this … so, so, so … thus it happened…"

Padre Pio looked at me and said: "But were you scandalized?"

"Well, a little bit, yes," I said, "… for a person who has been coming here to the convent for many years, who is always close to you, I was a little shocked."

And he said to me: "Look. If the Lord ever for a moment took his hand off my head and yours, we would do much worse. Tell him to come here and I will not treat him badly in front of everyone."

And so it was, of course.[100]

Sobering also was the story of another physician at the Casa Sollievo della Sofferenza, Dr. Giuseppe Sala:

"When I confessed the first time he sent me away and told me to come back after a month. He did the same to my wife who, unlike me, not very calmly accepted the suggestion and went back to confession to Padre Pio after four days. All the other times he treated me in confession with much fatherly concern and affability. Even with other people I could experience the great effectiveness of their contact with him in the confessional. I remember the episode of Prof. Rosario Scalabrino, a teacher at the University of Milan, who was strongly anticlerical. He came to see me in San Giovanni Rotondo because he wanted to confess to Padre Pio. To my amazement I took him to see the Padre and he did confess. I saw him again soon after, and he expressed gratitude and joy for the meeting with Padre Pio. Three days later he died."[101]

The method changed as needed, but the feelings of the confessor were always the same: horror at sin and love for the sinner. This is borne out by the testimony of this woman:

"I knelt in front of Padre Pio, my heart pounding. I was confused; I didn't understand anything but the final cutting and harsh words with which I was driven out of the confessional. I understood them very well. It was a beneficial blow that I will never forget. Later, a young man went to Padre Pio to intercede for me. And he said: 'What do you think? That I have a heart of stone? I did it for her own good. She left and my blessing will accompany her always.' After having lived nine years in peace since, I am grateful to have been chased away from his confessional back then."[102]

This final statement is from one of the Capuchin's penitents, whose word has assumed even greater authority because of the role to which the Holy Spirit called him. It is St. John Paul II, who wrote:

"During confession Padre Pio was shown as a confessor who had a simple and clear discernment and who treated the penitent with great love."[103]

The Objective was a Change of Life

A change of life in the confessional, then, more than in any other area of his life and mission and, in particular, of his priestly ministry, was the goal in which Padre Pio turned out to be an icon, the "Cyrenian carrying the cross of many, thus fulfilling the saying of the Apostle: 'Supply and perfect what is lacking in the passion of Christ,'"[104] as he himself put it. There's an expression that comes up again and again in conversations between Padre Pio and his penitents: "How much you cost me!" And even his confreres were reminded several times that "souls are acquired for God through sacrifice and penance."[105]

He felt himself to be "almost a third party in the dialogue between God and the sinner,"[106] as evidenced by the strong expression used in a letter to his spiritual director:

"What about the brothers? Alas! How many times, if not all the time, have I not had to say to God, the Judge, along with Moses: Forgive this people, or remove me from the book of life."[107]

It seems clear from the above described episodes that this singular confessor did not weigh on the scales the severity of the sins committed. He knew that sin, all sin, marks a rift in the relationship of love between man and God. "I'd much rather death," he wrote, "instead of deliberately deciding to offend a good God, Yes."[108] And he wanted to instil the same awareness in the hearts of those who demanded his pardon. "That's why Padre Pio was very demanding in requiring serious preparation for sacramental confession: as the witnesses who testify about this trial all agree. Since he wished that the penitent truly undertake a new life that would go well beyond a simple resolution, he wanted through the examination of conscience that the penitent not so much enter into the severity of the individual sin, as in the situation of the person who was refusing an offer of love that could be decisive for his or her existence."[109] This explains his great severity in "instilling in his penitents the hatred of sin"[110] and his use of strong language. When a young man, "tired and disappointed in life and in the way he was living it," said, "Padre, help me; I need your prayers. Help me to sin less often," the Capuchin snapped and replied, almost shouting: "Young man, you will not sin any more, do you understand? 'Sin less' does not exist. Sin is the death of the soul."[111] On another occasion, after listening to the guilt confessed by a sinner, he said, "You are singing a hymn to Satan while Jesus, out of his passionate love, broke his neck for you!"[112] Shock therapy though it was, it proved to be effective: "Often the penitent came out of the confessional crying, profoundly aware of the death situation in which he had found himself."[113]

In this perspective, the sinful act itself not only assumed a relative, even if severe importance, in Padre Pio's eyes but it could become an instrument of God's mercy. "Even the same sins, from which God in his goodness keeps us at a distance," he wrote to a spiritual daughter, "by his divine providence are ordered to the good of those who serve him. If the holy King

David had not sinned, would he have ever acquired such deep humility; or would Mary Magdalene have so ardently loved Jesus had he not forgiven her many sins, and Jesus would not have been able to forgive her, if she had not committed them?"[114]

Sin, then, according to the stigmatized Capuchin friar, can be an instrument of death[115] or of humility.[116] What makes the difference is only the attitude of the sinner. It's up to him or her to choose. And, when repentance and the intention to abandon the path of egoism were sincere, the friar became the icon of the paternal love of the Lord. "The mercy of God, my son," he says to a penitent out of breath, panting, who knocked on the grate of the confessional, "infinitely surpasses your malice."[117]

From that moment on, "Padre Pio was truly the traveling companion of those who came to him for confession"[118] and confession became a means of spiritual direction or the critical first step for the beginning of such a guided tour.

This was, therefore, the basic attitude that transformed the stigmatized Capuchin from being a simple confessor into an evangelizer through the confessional, into the dispenser of the mercy of the Lord. Not his charismatic gifts.

John Paul II, in his homily at the canonization Mass of Padre Pio, pointed out:

"The ministry of the confessional, which is one of the hallmarks of his apostolate, attracted great crowds of faithful to the monastery of San Giovanni Rotondo. Even when that unusual confessor treated pilgrims with apparent severity, the latter, becoming aware of the seriousness of sin and sincerely repentant, almost always came back for the peaceful embrace of sacramental forgiveness."[119]

He added this wish:

"May his example encourage priests to carry out with joy and zeal this ministry, so important even today."[120]

Conversions Continue

Padre Pio said of himself: "I will make more noise dead than alive." When he spoke these words he did not think certainly just about the persecution and slander that were unfinished with the end of his earthly journey nor with the official recognition of his holiness on the part of the Church. His prophetic vision looked also to the extraordinary action of grace that radiates from the urn that holds his mortal body, around which, every year, some seven million people kneel: people praying, participating in Masses, receiving Holy Communion, and approaching the sacrament of Reconciliation.

Today Padre Pio's mission is carried on by his confreres. And so we find that the pardon which was granted by the Lord to this place lost in southern Italy continues through the stigmatized saint.

For several years the Capuchin Order of Friars Minor, in the spring-summer-autumn period, send to San Giovanni Rotondo priests from different parts of the world to help those in the local fraternity hear confessions, especially in foreign languages.

A Friar Achylles Chiappin, Brazilian, happened to give absolution to a man "from a country far from Europe." For obvious reasons he could not add other details. "This man had killed eleven people in his life in the underworld. Then something clicked in him. Something that had never been revealed or which remained buried in the secrecy of confession. This something, however, brought him up to Padre Pio's church on the Gargano, to ask the friar: 'How can I repair the great harm I have caused to the families of the people I killed?'."

Even Friar Josué Flores Fernando Gamboa, of Silos, in Colombia, "had similar experiences. For example there was the one about a compatriot, a Colombian, who accidentally knelt in his confessional. The confession had begun in Italian. Then, having discovered their common origin, the two continued to talk in their own language. The penitent told about his dissolute life and about the beginning of a journey to change. It was only a vague resolution. Meanwhile he continued to live by selling drugs. Until one day 'he was stopped by the police when he only had with him a bag full of white powder.' It could have been the beginning of the end. The prison certainly would not have favored his plans for conversion. In fact, he probably would have turned into a hardened criminal. Instead, 'while the police were searching, the envelope with the drug fell to the ground and, on top of it, landed an image of Padre Pio that he had with him, covering the drug.' His narrow escape and the way in which it managed to save him from arrest caused his final choice to mature."[121] The choice of a radical conversion.

After exposure to these testimonies we can say, with documented certainty, that Padre Pio was a saint who achieved miracles. But, when we say that, we will not think any more about the inexplicable cures, which also continued to occur. We will not think of the "Casa Sollievo della Sofferenza," which many rightly called the "miracle of love" which also continues to regenerate many bodies and spirits affected by disease. Mainly our thoughts go to the very many souls who find God here and not health and earthly life, which in any case, sooner or later they will end up losing. And we give thanks to God for this man who agreed to be, for 58 years, a "carbon copy" of God's Son on the cross.

Notes for Chapter I

1. "Padre Pio's letter to Padre Benedetto da San Marco in Lamis, June 3, 1919," in P. da Pietrelcina, [Letters] *Epistolario*, M. Pobladura, from A. da Ripabottoni A. (Ed.), Edizioni Padre Pio da Pietrelcina, San Giovanni Rotondo (FG) 1995, vol. I, p. 1145.

2. The first "brief" news, unsigned, about Padre Pio was published on May 9, 1919, less than eight months after September 20, 1918, when the permanent stigmata appeared on the body of the Capuchin friar, age thirty-one, (cf. Anonymous, "The 'miracles' of a Capuchin in S. Giovanni Rotondo" in *Il Giornale d'Italia*, the nineteenth year, no. 123, May 9, 1919, fourth edition).

3. "Padre Pio's letter to Padre Benedetto of June 3, 1919," in *Letters*, op. cit., Vol. I, p. 1145.

4. Starting in 1908, following the provisions of the Holy See, Philosophy was called Lyceum. Cf. G. da San Giovanni Rotondo, "Notes on the life of Padre Pio from the novitiate to Sacred Eloquence," CP, XLV, pp. 9665-9671, in M. Iafelice, "The fraternity of the Capuchin monastery and the town of Serracapriola during the stay of Padre Pio in the year of 1907-1908." Attempts at an historical reconstruction were made in *Studies on Padre Pio*, Year X, no. 1, January-April 2009, p. 91.

5. Cf. "Letter of Padre Agostino da San Marco in Lamis to Padre Pio of 27 May 1909" in A. da San Marco in Lamis, *Diario*, Edizioni Padre Pio da Pietrelcina, San Giovanni Rotondo (FG) 2012, p. 317.

6. I. da Teano, "My thoughts on Padre Pio of Pietrelcina," in F. Riese Pio X, *Padre Pio, crucified without a cross*, Edizioni Padre Pio da Pietrelcina, San Giovanni Rotondo (FG) 2007, p. 73.

7. See ibid, p. 74; A. da Ripabottoni, "Life of the Servant of God Padre Pio of Pietrelcina of the Capuchin Friars Minor," in *Beatificationis et Canonizationis Servi Dei Pii a Pietrelcina*. *Positio super virtutibus*, Tipolitografia Signum, Bollate (MI) 1997, vol. III/1, p. 83.

8. *Beatificationis et Canonizationis Servi Dei Pii a Pietrelcina*. *Positio super virtutibus*, vol. IV, Section III, Tipografia Favia, Bari 1997, p. 71.

9. Cf. A. da Ripabottoni, *Padre Pio da Pietrelcina*. *Un Cireneo per tutti*, the Franciscan Cultural Centre, Foggia, 1974, p. 100.

10. Cf. B. da San Marco in Lamis, "Cronistoria di P. Pio," in F. Castelli, *"Padre Pio sotto inchiesta. L'autobiografia segreta"* [The "secret autobiography"] Edizioni Ares, Milano 2008, p. 291.

11. Cf. G. Di Flumeri, *Il Beato Padre Pio a Serracapriola*, Edizioni Padre Pio da Pietrelcina, San Giovanni Rotondo (FG) 2000, pp. 31-32. Some authors argue that the time that Fra Pio spent in the convent of Serracapriola during the school year 1907-1908 lasted only two months, because his health led the superiors to have him return to Pietrelcina. But such statements are not confirmed by any "archival documents." (Cf. M. Iafelice, *La Fraternità del convento dei Cappuccini e il paese di Serracapriola*, op. cit., p. 78).

12. Padre Agostino da San Marco in Lamis, aka Michele Daniele, was born in San Marco in Lamis, in the province of Foggia, January 9, 1880. He put on the Capuchin habit on August 19, 1897 and, after his novitiate, he was sent by his superiors in the religious province of Tuscany to undertake higher ecclesiastical studies. He was ordained on March 15, 1903 and, after returning in the Religious Province of Foggia, he followed specialized courses in Greek and French in public schools and won the competition within the Order for the Chair of Philosophy. He was Provincial Minister for nine years. He died in San Giovanni Rotondo May 14, 1963.

13. Cf. "Letter of Padre Agostino to Fra Pio of May 27, 1909," in A. da San Marco in Lamis, *Diario*, op. cit., p. 318.

14. Cf. "Letter of Padre Agostino to Fra Pio of May 28, 1909," ibid, pp. 319-320.

15. Bishop Benedetto, known as Pompe dei conti Bonazzi, Cassinese Benedictine was born in Naples on October 12, 1840; at the age of seven he entered the Benedictine school of the Trinity in Cava dei Tirreni. He was ordained on December 19, 1883 and, two years later, he graduated

in literature from the University of Naples where he taught literature. He gave his name to the Greek-Italian Dictionary, which he published in 1880. On March 7, 1894 he was elected ordinary abbot of the Benedictine community of Cava dei Tirreni, and on June 9, 1902, he was appointed archbishop of Benevento (Cf. *Annuario Pontificio*, 1911, p. 127). He died April 23, 1915 without having been made a cardinal.

16. Cf. "Padre Agostino Letter to Fra Pio of 30 May 1909," in A. da San Marco in Lamis, *Diario*, op. cit., p. 320.
17. Cf. "Padre Agostino Letter to Fra Pio of May 27, 1909," in ibid, p. 318.
18. Cf. G. Di Flumeri, *Il Beato Padre Pio da Pietrelcina*, Edizioni Padre Pio da Pietrelcina, San Giovanni Rotondo (FG) 2001, p. 21.
19. Born in Morcone on April 3, 1837, in 1893 he was appointed auxiliary bishop of Telese Cerreto and titular bishop of Thermopylae. In 1909 he was 72 years old and was "domiciled at home" (Cf. *Annuario Pontificio*, 1909).
20. Cf. M. Iafelice, *La Fraternità del convento dei Cappuccini e il paese di Serracapriola*, op. op. cit., pp. 80-81.
21. G. Di Flumeri, "The long pilgrimage of 1909," in *Voce di Padre Pio*, year VIII, no. 10, October 1977, p. 13.
22. Padre Benedetto da San Marco in Lamis, born Gerardo Giuseppe Nardella, was born in San Marco in Lamis, in the province of Foggia on March 16, 1872. While attending vocational schools in the capital city he felt a religious vocation and on December 11 in 1890 he took the Capuchin habit in the Morcone novitiate. He finished his studies in the religious province of Tuscany. He was ordained a priest on April 11, 1898, and soon after, he won the internal competition of the Order to teach philosophy and physics. He ruled the religious Province of Foggia from February 1908 to July 1919. He was sent as a General Visitator to the religious provinces of Bari-Lecce and Messina. From May 1920 to November 1921 he was deputy director and spiritual director of the International College "St. Lawrence of Brindisi" of the Friars Minor Capuchin. He died in San Severo on July 22, 1942.
23. "Letter of Padre Benedetto to Fra Pio of January 2, 1910," in *Collected Letters*, op. op. cit., Vol. I, p. 177. The Congregation for Religious, September 7, 1909, had established that in particular situations ecclesiastical studies made privately could be considered valid for the purpose of priestly ordination.

24. According to the canonical norms in force at the time it was necessary to be at least 24 years old.
25. Cf. "Letter of Padre Benedetto to Fra Pio of January 22, 1910," in *Collected Letters*, op. op. cit., Vol. I, p. 178.
26. Cf. "Letter of Padre Benedetto to Fra Pio of March 14, 1910," in *Collected Letters*, op. op. cit., Vol. I, p. 180.
27. Fra Pio of Pietrelcina studied books on sacred scripture, dogmatic theology, moral theology, spiritual theology, homiletics, secular history, Italian, French and Greek grammar, Italian vocabulary, two courses in Latin and one in Greek, some classics and other works, magazines and periodicals. But this list, already published in some detail, is partial because other texts were not preserved (cf. G. Di Flumeri, "I libri di studio di Padre Pio," in *Voce di Padre Pio*, no. IV, nos. 7- 8, July-August 1973, pp. 24 et seq.).
28. Cf. "Letter of Fra Pio to Padre Benedetto of May 26, 1910" in *Collected Letters*, op. op. cit., Vol. I, pp. 182-183. Cf. Also p. 183, n. 3.
29. "Letter from Fra Pio to Padre Benedetto of Mar. 14, 1910," in *Collected Letters*, op. cit., Vol. I, p. 180.
30. Cf. ibid.
31. "Letter from Fra Pio to Padre Benedetto of May 26, 1910," in *Collected Letters*, op. cit., Vol. I, p. 182.
32. Cf. "Letter of Fra Pio to Padre Benedetto of June 20, 1910," in *Collected Letters*, op. cit., Vol. I, p. 185.
33. Cf. "Letter of Fra Pio to Padre Benedetto of July 6, 1910," in *Collected Letters*, op. cit., Vol. I, p. 187.
34. "Letter of Padre Benedetto to Padre Pio of July 6, 1910," in *Collected Letters*, op. cit., Vol. I, p. 188.
35. See *Positio super virtutibus*, op. cit , Vol. III / 1, p. 90.
36. "Letter of Padre Benedetto to Fra Pio of July 6, 1910," in *Collected Letters*, op. cit., Vol. I, p. 188.
37. "Letter of Fra Pio to Padre Benedetto of July 22, 1910," in *Collected Letters*, op. cit., Vol. I, p. 190.
38. Cf. ibid 2.
39. Ibid, p. 191.
40. "Letter of Padre Benedetto to Fra Pio of July 26, 1910," in *Collected Letters*, op. cit., Vol. I, p. 191.
41. Cf. ibid, p. 192.

42. Don Salvatore Maria Pannullo was born in Pietrelcina on January 7, 1849; he became a priest at the age of 23, graduated in "Literature" and taught at the "Giannone" College and Seminary of Benevento, also becoming the spiritual director of the seminarians. In 1883 he was transferred to the diocesan seminary of Catanzaro as a professor and spiritual director. He returned to his hometown at age 52, when he was appointed parish priest of Pietrelcina. He took canonical possession of the parish on October 24, 1901. Francesco Forgione served him as an altar boy until he entered the novitiate of the Capuchin Friars at Morcone (cf. L. da Prata, A. da Ripabottoni, *Beata te Pietrelcina*, Capuchin Friars, Pietrelcina (BN) 1994, pp. 91 et seq. and p. 134).

43. Cf. "Letter of Fra Pio to Padre Benedetto of July 29, 1910," in *Collected Letters*, op. cit., Vol. I, p. 193.

44. Cf. "Letter of Fra Pio to Padre Benedetto of July 31, 1910," in *Collected Letters*, op. cit., Vol. I, p. 194.

45. Monsignor Paolo Schinosi was born in Benevento of April 4, 1827. On April 19, 1897 he was appointed titular bishop of Gaza and on February 20, 1901 he was promoted to titular archbishop of Marcianopolis (Cf. *Annuario Pontificio*, 1903, p. 438).

46. Cf. "Certificate of priestly ordination," in *Positio super virtutibus*, op. cit., Vol. III / 1, p. 93.

47. Cf. "Letter of Padre Pio to Padre Benedetto of July 31, 1910," in *Collected Letters*, op. cit., Vol. I, p. 194.

48. Cf. F. Grassi, L. Ingaldi, *Pastors of the Cathedral of Benevento*, Tipografia "Auxiliatrix," Benevento 1969, p. 180.

49. Cf. Pio of Pietrelcina, *Letters*, op. cit., Vol. I, p. 192, n. 1.

50. "Letter of Padre Pio to Padre Benedetto of April 1911," in *Collected Letters*, op. cit., Vol. I, p. 218. Padre Pio will come back to this matter at least three more times (Cf. "Letter of Padre Pio to Padre Benedetto of January 5, 1912," in *Collected Letters*, op. cit., Vol. I, p. 246; "Letter of Padre Pio to Padre Benedetto of Mar. 2, 1912, "in ibid, p. 262. "Letter of Padre Pio to Padre Benedetto of Mar. 15, 1913, "in ibid, p. 345).

51. "Letter of Padre Benedetto's to Padre Pio of April 12, 1911," in ibid, p. 221.

52. "Letter of Padre Benedetto to Padre Pio of March 16, 1913," in ibid, 348. Cf. Also "Letter of Padre Benedetto to Padre Pio of March 4, 1912," in ibid, p. 263. Not even the mediation of Padre Agostino da

San Marco in Lamis manages to change Padre Benedetto's mind (cf. "Letter of Padre Agostino to Padre Pio of January 18, 1912," in ibid, p. 254; "Letter of Padre Agostino to Padre Pio of February 1, 1912," in ibid, p. 257; "Letter of Padre Agostino to Padre Pio of February 27, 1913," in ibid, p. 341; "Letter of Padre Agostino to Padre Pio of March 15, 1913," in ibid, p. 346; "Letter of Padre Agostino to Padre Pio of April 9, 1913," in ibid, p. 355).

53. Cf. L. Dimatteo, "Padre Pio and the faculty to hear confessions," in *Studies on Padre Pio*, year II, no. 2, May-August 2001, pp. 163-164.

54. "Letter of Padre Benedetto to Padre Pio of October 4, 1911" in *Letters*, op. cit., Vol. I, p. 239.

55. "Letter of Padre Benedetto to the Minister General of the Friars Minor Capuchin of December 4, 1911," in G. Saldutto, " Un giovane sacerdote di angelici costumi," in *Voce di Padre Pio*, Year V, n. 3, March 1974, p. 4.

56. "Letter of Padre Benedetto to Padre Pio of December 17, 1913," in *Collected Letters*, op. cit., Vol. I, p. 438.

57. "Letter of Padre Agostino to Padre Pio of November 2, 1914," in ibid, pp. 499-500.

58. Cf. "Letter of Padre Agostino to Padre Pio of February 4, 1915," in ibid, p. 528.

59. Cf. "Letter of Padre Benedetto to Padre Pio of December 24, 1915," in ibid, p. 709.

60. Cf. "Padre Agostino's Letter to Padre Pio of January 29, 1916" in ibid, pp. 727-728. Padre Pio already knew a few days before his entry into the friary that his ministry would be a fight against evil. Francesco Forgione, the future Padre Pio, was then 15 years old when he experienced an inner struggle between the strong "vocation to the religious state" and "the vanity of this world." At that time the Lord made him understand clearly his will through a vision "perceived with the eye of the mind." The boy found himself, suddenly, next to "a stately man of rare beauty, shining like the sun. He took his hand and said, 'Come with me, because you'll need to fight like a brave warrior.' He led him into a very large open space. There was there a great multitude of men; they were divided into two groups. On the one hand he saw handsome men dressed in white robes as white as the snow; on the other hand where there was the second group, he saw horrid looking men

dressed in black in the likeness of dark shadows." While Francis was watching these two groups of men, "suddenly down the middle of the space that divided the two groups came a man of immense height with a horrible face, similar to that of an Ethiopian and whose forehead touched the clouds. When this strange figure reached him, the man who held him by the hand said to the youth: 'You must fight with that individual!' At these words the boy turned pale. He was about to faint with fright if his guide had not supported him by the arm. He only found the courage to ask his majestic companion to be saved from "the wrath of that very strange figure" who seemed "so strong that all the men in the world put together would not be enough to knock him down." But the response was more peremptory than the first two calls, "Vain is all your resistence; it is necessary to come to blows with him. Take heart: enter the battle confidently, advancing boldly, and I will stand behind you; I will help and will not let him knock you down; as the victory prize that you will receive I will give you a beautiful crown to put on your head. There is no other choice." Francis entered "into combat with that formidable and mysterious character," and, with the help of his brilliant companion, who would not leave him alone even for an instant, in the end defeated him and forced him to flee. His guide then, faithful to his promise, took out "from under his clothes a rare beautiful crown which it would be vain to try to describe," and put it on his head, but immediately he took it off again, saying: "I had kept one more beautiful than this laid up for you if you knew how to fight the good fight with that character with whom you fought just now." To this, moreover, the handsome and majestic man added another promise: "I will always be at your side; I will always help you, so that you will always manage to crush him." The vision ended with the "flight between screams, curses and shouts on the part" of those horrid giants with dark faces and with the praise of the men wearing white robes "for that man more splendid and beautiful than the sun." (Cf. Pio of Pietrelcina, "Autobiographical Notes," in Collected Letters, op. cit., vol. I, pp. 1280 et seq.).

61. Cf. L. Di Matteo, "Padre Pio and the Faculty to Hear Confessions," in Studies on Padre Pio, from May-August 2001, pp. 170 et seq.

62. John Paul II, Homily at the Mass of Beatification of Padre Pio of Pietrelcina, 2 May 1999, 3.

63. Benedict XVI, Speech given at the meeting with the priests, men and women religious and young people during his pastoral visit to San Giovanni Rotondo, June 21, 2009.
64. "Letter of Card. Donato Sbarretti, Secretary of the Holy Office, to the Minister General of the Friars Minor Capuchin of May 23, 1931," in *Positio super virtutibus*, op. cit., Vol. III/1, p. 428. The original text in Latin is: "Patri Pio a Pietrelcina omnes auferantur facultates ministeriales, excepta tantum facultate s. Missam celebrandi, sed intra dumtaxat septa monasterii, in sacello interiori, privatim, non in ecclesia publica."
65. "Letter of the Attorney General of the Order of Friars Minor Capuchins, Fra Lazarus da Arbonne, to the Provincial Minister of the Capuchin of Foggia, Padre Bernardo d'Alpicella of July 14, 1933," in ibid, p. 439.
66. Cf. "Provisions promulgated by the Provincial Minister of the Friars Minor Capuchin of the Religious Province of Foggia, Padre Bernardo d'Alpicella, of March 25, 1934," in ibid, p. 448.
67. Cf. "Letter from the Provincial Minister, Padre Bernardo d'Alpicella, the Guardian of the Convent of San Giovanni Rotondo of May 12, 1934" in ibid, p. 453. In reality, the Minister General of the Order had already obtained in March "a benign disposition" from the Holy Office to permit "Padre Pio to hear sacramental confessions 'utriusque sexus'" that is, of both sexes (Cf. "Letter of the Minister General of the Order of Friars Minor Capuchin, Fra Vigilio da Valstagna, to the Provincial Minister of Foggia, Padre Bernardo d'Alpicella of March 19, 1934," in ibid, p. 447), but the Provincial Minister immediately granted to the stigmatized Friar the right to confess men as well (Cf. "Dispositions promulgated by the Provincial Minister of the Friars Minor Capuchin of the Religious Province of Foggia, Padre Bernardo d'Alpicella on March 25, 1934," in ibid, p. 448) and only in May to also include women.
68. G. Festa, *Misteri di scienza e luci di fede. Le stigmate del Padre Pio da Pietrelcina*, Stabilimento Tipo-Litografico Vittorio Ferri, Rome 1938², pp. 195 et seq.
69. Cf. F. Guarino, "Alberto Del Fante, spiritual son of Padre Pio and author," in *Studies on Padre Pio*, year X, no. 1, January-April 2009, p. 110.

70. A. Del Fante, *From Doubt to Faith*, Constantine Galleri, Bologna 1931, pp. 7 et seq.

71. A. Del Fante, *Per la Storia*. *Padre Pio da Pietrelcina il primo sacerdote stigmatizzato*, Galleri Editore, Bologna 1932, pp. 149 et seq.

72. G. Caradonna, "La Testimonianza di un onorevole," in *Archivio Padre Pio*, fg. 1.

73. Cf. P. Bruni, *Giuseppe Caradonna and the National Right*, Serarcangeli, Rome 1996, pp. 109 et seq.

74. Cf. G. Caradonna, "La Testimonianza di un onorevole," op. cit., fg. 2.

75. Anonymous, "A Known Bolognese Communist converts in front of Padre Pio," in *Giornale dell'Emilia*, May 24, 1950. Cf. also Anonymous, "The secretary of the U.D.I. abjures communist past," in *Il Giornale d'Italia*, May 24, 1950; Anonymous, "The UDI secretary of Bologna converted by Padre Pio Pietrelcina," in the afternoon May 23, 1950, latest edition; C. Trabucco, "In the presence of Padre Pio the agitator finds the light," in *L'Avvenire d'Italia*, June 8, 1950; Anonymous, "The UDI secretary of Bologna converted to the faith by Padre Pio," in *Gazetta Sera*, May 23-24, latest edition; Anonymous, "Communist Teacher converted by Padre Pio," in *L'Avvenire d'Italia*, May 24, 1950; M. Drusiani, "His professor companion turned from Marx to Christ," *Oggi*, year VI, no. 23, June 8, 1950; M. Ciampi, "A member of the communist hierarchy is converted in the presence of Padre Pio of Piretralcina [sic]," in *La voce del parroco*, anno XXII. n. 6, giugno 1950, p. 3.

76. Cf. G. Bardazzi, *Un discepolo di Padre Pio*, stampato in proprio, Scandicci (FI), 2007, pp. 18-19.

77. Ibid, p. 37.

78. Ibid, p. 20.

79. Ibid, p. 24.

80. Cf. pp. 30 et seq.

81. Cf. pp. 37 et seq.

82. E. Notte, *Padre Pio e padre Eusebio. Briciole di storia*, Grafiche Grilli, Foggia 2007, pp. 155 et seq.

83. "Letter of Padre Pio to Padre Benedetto of November 20, 1921," in *Collected Letters*, op. cit., Vol. I, p. 1247.

84. C. da Sessano, *Testimonianza su Padre Pio*, Edizioni Padre Pio da Pietrelcina, San Giovanni Rotondo (FG) 2000, p. 10.

85. Ibid.

86. A. da Ripabottoni, *Padre Pio racconta e dice*, Edizioni Padre Pio da Pietrelcina, San Giovanni Rotondo (FG) 2005, p. 446.

87. C. Capobianco, *Detti e aneddoti di Padre Pio*, Edizioni Padre Pio da Pietrelcina, San Giovanni Rotondo (FG) 1996, p. 54.

88. L. Lotti, "Padre Pio da Pietrelcina: la dimensione pedagogica della riconciliazione," in *Studi su Padre Pio*, anno VII, n. 1 gennaio-aprile 2006, p. 135.

89. P. Funicelli, *Padre Pio tra sandali e cappuccio*, Angelo Maria Mischitelli (Ed.), Leone Editrice, Foggia 2006, pp. 302-303.

90. Cf. P. Funicelli, "Arciconfraternita della buona morte," in *Voce di Padre Pio*, anno XII, n. 12, dicembre 1981, pp. 12 et seq.

91. "Testimonianza di padre Carmelo Durante da Sessano del Molise," in *Canonizationis Servi Dei Pii a Pietrelcina. Positio super virtutibus*, vol. II, Bollate (MI), Tipolitografia Signum, 1994, p. 785.

92. M. Castoro, Homily on the Feast of St. Pio of Pietrelcina, September 23, 2011, 2.

93. A. da Ripabottoni, *Padre Pio racconta e dice*, op. cit., p. 445.

94. Ibid.

95. Cf. L. Lotti, " Padre Pio da Pietrelcina: la dimensione pedagogica della riconciliazione," in *Studi su Padre Pio*, anno VII, n. 1 gennaio-aprile 2006, p. 142.

96. M. Castoro, Homily on the Feast of St. Pio of Pietrelcina, op. cit.

97. L. Lotti, "Padre Pio da Pietrelcina: la dimensione pedagogica della riconciliazione", in *Studi su Padre Pio*, anno VII, n. 1 gennaio-aprile 2006, p. 134.

98. "Testimony of Sister Maria Francesca Consolata" in *Positio super virtutibus*, op. cit., Vol. II, p. 1191.

99. San Giovanni Rotondo (n.d.a.).

100. Interview given by Professor Francesco Lotti, author, April 29, 2006.

101. "Testimony of Dr. Giuseppe Sala" in *Positio super virtutibus*, op. cit., Vol. II, p. 740.

102. "Testimonianza di Emma Dell'Orto", in V. da Casacalenda (Ed.), *Padre Pio da Pietrelcina. Testimonianze*, Edizioni Padre Pio da Pietrelcina, San Giovanni Rotondo (FG) 1970, p. 90.

103. S. Campanella, *The Pope and the Friar*, Edizioni Padre Pio da Pietrelcina, San Giovanni Rotondo (FG) 2007, p. 34.

104. "Letter of Padre Pio to Padre Agostino of May 8, 1919," in *Collected Letters*, op. cit., Vol. I, p. 1277.

105. L. Lotti, "Padre Pio da Pietrelcina: la dimensione pedagogica della riconciliazione," in *Studi su Padre Pio*, anno VII, n. 1 gennaio-aprile 2006, p. 133.

106. Ibid.

107. "Letter of Padre Pio to Padre Benedetto of November 20, 1921," in *Collected Letters*, op. cit., Vol. I, p. 1247.

108. "Letter of Padre Pio to Padre Benedetto of July 6, 1919," in *Collected Letters*, op. cit., Vol. I, p. 187.

109. L. Lotti, "Padre Pio da Pietrelcina: la dimensione pedagogica della riconciliazione," in *Studi su Padre Pio*, anno VII, n. 1 gennaio-aprile 2006, op. cit., p. 137.

110. "Testimony of Joan Rizzani" in *Positio super virtutibus*, op. cit., Vol. II, p. 100.

111. Cf. A. da Ripabottoni, *Padre Pio racconta e dice*, op. cit., p. 380.

112. Ibid, p. 377.

113. L. Lotti, "Padre Pio da Pietrelcina: la dimensione pedagogica della riconciliazione," in *Studi su Padre Pio*, anno VII, n. 1 gennaio-aprile 2006, op. cit., p. 136.

114. "Letter of Padre Pio to Antoinette Vona on November 15, 1917," in Pio of Pietrelcina, *Letters*, op. cit., Vol. III, pp. 823-824.

115. Cf. Mt 25:41-46.

116. Cf. 2 Corinthians 12:7.

117. A. da Ripabottoni, *Padre Pio racconta e dice*, op. cit., p. 374.

118. L. Lotti, "Padre Pio da Pietrelcina: la dimensione pedagogica della riconciliazione," in *Studi su Padre Pio*, anno VII, n. 1 gennaio-aprile 2006, op. cit., p. 133.

119. John Paul II, Homily at the Mass of canonization of Padre Pio of Pietrelcina, June 16, 2002, 3.

120. Ibid.

121. C. Vicedomini, "Friars from all over the world," in *Voce di Padre Pio*, XXXIV year, n. 10, October 2003, p. 52.

Chapter II

THE CHARISMS OF PADRE PIO
A GIFT OF GOD'S MERCY

Rarely in the history of the Church are the biographies of saints so characterized by a multitude of charisms, with wide confirmation through multiple converging testimonies, as happened in the case of St. Pio of Pietrelcina. Without emphasizing supernatural events that can sometimes lead to forms of expression of faith in danger of being contaminated by elements of superstition or fanaticism, but without even a preliminary attitude of ostracism of genuine forms of popular piety, it is expedient to seriously reflect on what the Lord has freely done in the life of Padre Pio through a synthesis of various phenomena and, above all, to try to hypothesize their function as part of the mission entrusted to this holy Capuchin to dispense divine mercy in our time.

Miracles

In the collective imagination, even of Catholics, the term "holy" immediately calls to mind the concept of miracles. And the miracles ascribed to the intercession of Padre Pio are many. Suffice it to say that, for over 45 years, the magazine *Voce di Padre Pio* has made public some of the many expressions of gratitude that come to the Capuchin friars for healings received. And many others are sure to be reported in the future since a now famous survey of *Famiglia Cristiana* places the stigmatized Capuchin in first place among the saints invoked by Italians.[1]

It was precisely the miracles of Padre Pio that attracted the attention of newspapers and encouraged the phenomenon of pilgrimages to San Giovanni Rotondo as soon as word spread that a friar with the stigmata lived there. Not surprisingly, scanning the first 20 titles dedicated to Padre Pio from as far back as May 9, 1919, when the first news appeared in *Il Giornale d'Italia*, in most cases the protagonists are the miracles themselves. "Many and diverse," wrote the unknown writer of the first text on Padre Pio published in a newspaper, "are the miraculous events attributed to the 'Saint'". A few weeks later, in the June 20-21 morning edition, *Il Mattino* led with the scoop: A miraculous healing took place before the eyes of the reporter, Renato Trevisani. This exceptional event prompted the daily newspaper of Naples to dedicate an entire page to him under the title "the man who works miracles." And in its summary announced: "Padre Pio, the 'Saint' of San Giovanni Rotondo, performs a miracle in the presence of our special envoy."

Thus, already in 1923, the British newspaper *The Observer* certified that "San Giovanni Rotondo has become a place of pilgrimage, where people flock from all over the world and more than one crowned head has traveled to the Apulian town to seek help and comfort from the 'Saint'". But then it added, as if in response to allegations that circulated on behalf of the Capuchin from Pietrelcina: "Padre Pio does not claim to have miraculous powers; he is the simplest and most modest of men. He has a mild, ascetic demeanor."

Many therefore have been the miracles attributed to this zealous religious, during his life and after his death. At present, however, in the prospect of being able to contribute to the realization of the project of Fra Gerardo Di Flumeri, who was the Vice-Postulator of the Cause for the Beatification and Canonization of Padre Pio, to establish in San Giovanni Rotondo a bureau based on the medical model in Lourdes, the only miracles that we can with certainty consider as having been obtained thanks to the mediation of the friar from Pietrelcina are two: one that allowed him to obtain the title of Blessed and another of which he was unaware that gave him the chance to be proclaimed a saint.

The first took place in early November 1995 at the Ospedali Riuniti of Salerno "St John of God and Ruggi d'Aragona." On the evening of October 31 Counselor De Martino, who at the time was 47 years old, felt "a twinge of pain in the retrosternal and left subclavian region with a general sense of unease, chills, body aches all over the body and a feeling of suffocation."[2] The next morning, noting "a swelling in her neck," she was accompanied to the emergency room where she was willingly hospitalized. After two attacks a diagnosis was made of "a rupture or laceration of the thoracic duct resulting in trauma with a massive effusion of lymphatic fluid, estimated at about two liters" and a surgical intervention was proposed as the only possible remedy.[3] Her first thought was to call San Giovanni Rotondo and ask Fra Modestino Fucci to have Padre Pio pray for her health. De Martino, in fact, was for several years devoted to the stigmatized friar. Her husband even entrusted himself to the intercession of the revered Capuchin, while her daughter and later her son reached Fra Modestino by telephone to strengthen their mother's request. Alarmed by the tone of voice of the children, the lay brother realized that the situation was serious. He left everything and went to the crypt to pray.[4]

Just after the second attack, as she was being accompanied to her room, the patient sensed in the elevator, "an intense perfume of flowers." But an even more significant event occurred "in the afternoon of November 3rd," when she had the sensation that someone "by themselves was sewing up her left collarbone." On the morning of November 4th she sensed "the smell" again.[5] Subsequent examinations showed her complete and instantaneous healing and the uselessness of going ahead with the already planned surgery. On November 12, 1997 Fra Gerardo Di Flumeri entrusted the whole dossier to the Postulator General of the Capuchins, Fra Paolino Rossi, for delivery to the Congregation for the Causes of Saints.

The examination of the documentation began in January of 1998. On April 30th the medical consultation of the Vatican Congregation unanimously judged "scientifically inexplicable"[6] the healing of the Counselor Mrs. De Martino. On June 22nd, with the unanimous consensus of the six theological consultors in favor, the event is described as a "miracle". These findings were also confirmed, on October 20th, by the cardinals, archbishops and bishops of the same Congregation. These three opinions made it possible for the Holy Father to approve, on December 21, 1998, the decree regarding the miracle attributed to the intercession of Padre Pio.[7]

The second miracle took place a few months after the beatification, in the intensive care unit of the "Casa Sollievo della Sofferenza." On the morning of January 20, 2000, Matteo Pio Colella, a seven year old child, was in the classroom of his school, in San Giovanni Rotondo, when he was suddenly seized with chills, high fever, drowsiness and mental disorientation. His teacher, Concetta Centra, immediately called his mother, Maria Lucia Ippolito, on her cellphone and she in turn phoned her husband, Antonio, a urologist on duty at the hospital founded by Padre Pio, who brought his son home and personally took care of him. Here the clinical picture worsened with headache, vomiting, reduced state of alertness and purple spots spreading all over his body. Even antipyretics could not bring down a fever that, indeed, increased up to 40.2° C. [104.36° F]. Because of this, in the evening, in consultation with a pediatrician friend of the family, Matteo Pio was transported to the hospital emergency room and was subject to all kinds of clinical exams.[8] When the report arrived, the doctors uttered a diagnosis that seemed like a condemnation: "Meningococcal sepsis, hyperacute septic shock, serious arterial hypotension, cardiac arrest, protracted hypoxemia, respiratory distress, disseminated intravascular coagulation, multi-organ failure."[9]

The little patient was immediately hospitalized in Intensive Care II where, during the night, he worsened interiorly, with "a progressive deterioration of vital functions, to an involvement of nine organs becoming simultaneously insufficient"[10] and, then, in the morning, to the dramatic moment of cardiac arrest, despite the therapy undertaken since 02:00 a.m. with dopamine and norepinephrine. At 9:30 it was necessary intubate him.[11] "The clinical conditions were desperate," Dr. Pietro Gerardo Violi, who personally followed the case, said explaining:

> "The child had generalized cyanosis and, despite assisted mechanical ventilation for an extended period of time until the oxygen reaches levels under 30%… The child presented serious heart failure with extreme bradycardia and acute pulmonary edema, and that aggravated the state of shock which spread also to the peripheral organs; it was only natural to assume that these conditions would lead to death or, at best, irreparable damage to vital organs."[12]

Not even the primary department head, Dr. Paolo De Vivo, was more optimistic, as he stated in his deposition:

> "Already in those moments I was convinced of the impossibility of success or at least I was convinced that […] brain and kidney damage would follow […]. The cardiac involvement as seen in the radiographs indicated the need for circulatory support with very high doses of adrenaline and noradrenaline (doses that would be very high even for an adult) convinced me of a possible sudden cardiac death or of heart diseases should the child survive. Personally, I have often thought that death could happen there at any moment. I admitted to myself and I expressed aloud with my staff on more than one occasion that I did not think a positive resolution was possible."[13]

Meanwhile, the mother entrusted him to Padre Pio and put together a real network of prayer, asking all those she knew to have recourse to the intercession of the blessed and to extend a chain invitation to others to do the same.

She herself, with the permission of the Friars spent all night and the early hours of the morning, between the tomb of the future saint and his cell.[14]

But, at about eleven o'clock, "suddenly" it happened: "something extraordinary and with the disbelief of all. His respiratory center, probably compromised by meningococcemia (the picture of his chest indicated acute pulmonary edema), resumed oxygenating the blood; his heart resumed its course, and blood pressure, spreading adequately throughout his organs, was detected. Any complications show a pattern of quick resolution."[15] His recovery was very rapid and, on February 6, the young patient was already fully awake and cooperative: he asked for PlayStation and surprised all the doctors who saw him interact with it confidently, dispelling their fear "of being faced with a child with mental and nervous deficits, [...] a fear that had a sound scientific basis." He was discharged, completely healed, on February 26. In April he went back "to school, showing more exuberance than usual and with an intellectural capacity that was amazing."[16]

During the canonical process, held at the Ecclesiastical Tribunal of the Archdiocese of Manfredonia-Vieste from 11 June to 17 October 2000, Matteo Pio recalled:

"I had heard of Padre Pio since I was a little child; Every Sunday my parents would take me to visit the tomb of Padre Pio.

I could not pray to Padre Pio during my sleep time, but as soon as I woke up I started to pray and to invoke Padre Pio.

Barely awake, I held her hand, looking for another hand and said: 'I want Padre Pio.' My mother did not understand me.

During sleep I was not alone, I saw an old man.

I saw an old man with a white beard and a long brown dress at a distance from this bed, through a round hole. I was close to some machinery and he gave me his right hand and said: 'Matteo, do not worry, you will get well soon' and he smiled at me."[17]

On the following October 23rd documentation about this cure was delivered to the Congregation for the Causes of Saints. On November 22, 2001 it passed the examination of the medical consultors with the unanimous judgment of "scientifically inexplicable."[18] On December 11th it passed that of the theological consultors and on the 18th of the same month it received a positive opinion from the Ordinary Session of the cardinals, archbishops and bishops of the Congregation.

Based on these opinions, Pope John Paul II, on December 20, 2001, promulgated the decree to declare "a miracle performed by God through the intercession of Blessed Pio of Pietrelcina (born Francesco Forgione), professed priest of the Order of Friars Minor Capuchin, namely the rapid, complete and lasting healing of the child Matteo Pio Colella from 'hyperacute meningococcal sepsis with septic shock, serious arterial hypotension, cardiac arrest, protracted hypoxemia, respiratory distress, disseminated intravascular coagulation, and multi-organ failure.'"[19]

But to obtain miracles from the Lord's mercy, as mentioned in the introduction of this chapter, was only one of many extraordinary gifts granted to Padre Pio.

The Stigmata

It is known to most Padre Pio devotees what occurred in the old church choir of the convent of San Giovanni Rotondo on the morning of September 20, 1918 since it has been narrated in detail in a letter, written while his memory was still "fresh," just a month after the event.

Here is the central part of the story:

> "On the morning of the 20th of last month, in the choir, after I had celebrated Mass I yielded to drowsiness similar to a sweet sleep. All internal and external senses, to say nothing of the same faculties of the soul, were at an indescribable peace. In all this there was total silence around and inside me. [...]
>
> And while all this was taking place, I saw before me a mysterious figure, similar to the one seen on the evening of August 5, which differed only in that his hands and feet and side were dripping blood.
>
> This sight terrified me and what I felt at that moment is indescribable. I thought I would die and would have died if the Lord had not intervened and strengthened my heart which was about to burst out of my chest.
>
> The vision disappeared and I became aware that my hands, feet and side were dripping blood."[20]

Only nearly three years later, in response to questions that were posed by his first apostolic visitor, Monsignor Raffaello Carlo Rossi, did the friar bring up an important detail regarding the experience of September 20, 1918: the mysterious man uttered a short phrase. Few words, but which clearly showed his identity and help us understand the meaning of what was going to happen: "I associate you with my passion."[21]

In fact even regarding this stigmatization[22] – it was neither the first nor the only one - we would know very little, if the wounded hands of Padre Pio had not been noticed by one of his spiritual daughters: Nina Campanile.[23] Here is her testimony:

"In presenting the offerings for the Mass I saw, on the back of the right hand of the Padre, in the center, a stigma. It seemed to me like a sunburn. I understood right away, but I pretended not to understand, and exclaimed: 'Oh, Padre! Have you burned your hand?' He turned pale and hid his hands behind his back. We continued to talk of other things; around sunset we came out of the sacristy. I joined my cousin, Nunziatina Campanile, and the Padre took us to the Little Chapel of St. Francis, which was then located half way to the Albergo Villa Pia…. In leaving, I tried to kiss his hand right on the stigma, but the Padre in pain exclaimed: 'If you knew what a humiliation this gives me!' But I said, 'Padre, for Christmas, by virtue of these stigmata, the Lord will grant us many graces!' 'Will they still be here until Christmas?' 'I will pray very hard to the Lord that he will take everything away!' the Padre added, and he went into the convent. As soon as I arrived home I told my mother … that the Padre had received the stigmata like St. Francis, and I conveyed the same news said to my sister Lucietta. In short order news about the stigmata spread all over."[24]

In vain, then, did Padre Pio try "to hide the signs of the passion within the sleeves of his habit by taking between his fingers the edges of the cape."[25] Word, by now, at least in San Giovanni Rotondo, had spread.

It was the same Nina Campanile who informed the superior of the convent, Padre Paolino da Casacalenda, who had not noticed anything. "Padre Paolino," she said, smiling and full of inner satisfaction, "did you know that Padre Pio received the stigmata?" The guardian friar began "laughing out loud," because he "absolutely did not believe that this had happened." He thought to himself: "Is it possible that Padre

Pio received the stigmata and here I, who was always with him, had not noticed?" "There's no need to laugh," she added, "because what I say is true. You yourself can ask the Padre or find other means to know the truth."

The next morning Padre Paolino went to see his confrere in his cell and entered "without knocking." Padre Pio was "sitting at his desk writing," but "got up right away … and remained standing with the stigmata covered." The superior asked him to sit down and added, "Go on writing, I pray, because this morning I have nothing special to say to you. I just came in to say hello and spend a few minutes with you before you start your lessons." Padre Pio obeyed and Padre Paolino could "see in front of him the wound in the back and on the palm of his right hand, and then the one in the back of the left." He could not see the one "in the palm of the left because he kept it on the desk to hold the sheet of paper still." It was enough.

The same day the local superior wrote "a letter to the Most Reverend Padre Benedetto … in San Marco La Catola, informing him of what had happened and inviting him to come as soon as possible to San Giovanni Rotondo not only to personally acquaint himself of the fact, but also to plan with him a course of action […]. Benedetto did not come […]. He wrote a letter in which it seemed that he did not give much importance to what had happened; he only recommended maintaining the greatest silence regarding it."[26]

For nearly a month Padre Pio did not write anything to Padre Benedetto who, besides being his major superior, as provincial minister, was also his spiritual director. Only on October 17th did he find the strength to take pen in hand to mention the incident, but with a vague and confusing narrative.

"I must utter my fiat looking at that mysterious person who wounds and does not desist from his harsh, bitter, sharp and penetrating work, nor does he give time to heal old wounds, but immediately opens up other new ones causing infinite agony to the poor victim?

Ah, my Padre, come to my aid, for goodness sake! My whole being is raining blood and I am forced to resign myself to see it pass even over my eyes. Ah! May this agony, this condemnation, this humiliation, this confusion cease!"[27]

At this point the Minister Provincial was alarmed and ordered him:

"My son, tell me everything and clearly, and without dissimulating. What does this mysterious figure do? Regarding the flow of blood, how many times per day or week does it take place? What happened to your hands and feet, and how? I want to know word for word everything under holy obedience."[28]

So only under "holy obedience" did the stigmatized friar, on October 22, 1918, recount in detail what had taken place on the preceding September 20th.[29] But he did so with great difficulty and without hiding his discomfort. "My God," one can still read in his letter of reply to Padre Benedetto, "what confusion and what humiliation I feel when I have to manifest what You have worked in this Your miserable creature!"[30]

This, however, was the second stigmatization, lasting until just before his death.

In fact the body of Padre Pio received the impression of the stigmata for the first time a few days or a few weeks after his ordination, which took place on August 10, 1910. Of this episode we have no certain date. At that time the friar was in Pietrelcina, to be precise under the elms of the Piana Romana, the part of the country where his parents had a farm for planting and grazing. These first stigmata "were visible," but because the soul of the young Capuchin "was very shocked by this phenomenon, he prayed to the Lord that such a visible phenomenon be taken away. From that time on they no longer appeared; even though the wounds disappeared, however, that did not mean that the acute pain went away as well."[31]

Again in this case Padre Pio did not have the courage to speak openly and immediately with Padre Benedetto. He did so in a letter dated September 8, 1911, in which he related:

> "Then last night something happened which I can neither explain nor understand. In the middle of the palms of my hands a red mark appeared about the size of a penny, accompanied also by a sharp and acute pain in the middle of the red marks. This pain was more pronounced in the middle of the left hand, so much so that I can still feel it. Even under my feet I can feel some pain.
>
> It is almost a year now that this phenomenon has been repeating itself, however it has been some time now that it has not repeated itself. Don't be upset that this is the first time I mention it to you; because I have always had to fight against the shame. Even now if you knew how much violence I had to do to myself to bring myself tell you this!"[32]

Therefore, when all is said and done, the holy Capuchin bore the signs of the crucifixion of Christ on his body for 58 years: first visibly, then invisibly, then visibly once again. And, it is even more significant because these signs lasted for the duration of his priestly ministry.

Once his mission was finished, the stigmata likewise disappeared. Of these wounds, which many had seen and that some had examined, no trace was found during the inspection performed on the corpse by Prof. Giuseppe Sala upon his death. There are photos documenting that the skin was perfectly smooth again as if there had never been any injuries, without even the hint of a scar. It was a phenomenon that, clinically, can be defined as "an extraordinary healing that represents a real leap from the natural course of events."[33] In fact, Dr. Paolo Maria Marianeschi, specialist in general surgery at the Surgical Clinic of the University of Perugia, during the first "Study Conference on the stigmata of the Servant of God Padre Pio of Pietrelcina"[34], stated that "deep skin lesions always heal with a scar […]. In humans, the scarring is a mandatory and not an optional process […]. It is necessarily and automatically triggered at the same time that the anatomical lesion of the tissue is produced. So the disappearance of the stigmata of Padre Pio or their healing without leaving a scar, say what you will, is a real pathophysiological absurdity."[35]

This last phenomenon is very important. It helps us not only to retain as prejudicial and of little scientific validity any explanation of the stigmata of the Capuchin of Pietrelcina different from the supernatural, but it also helps us to better understand the significance of those wounds.

On the body of Padre Pio there appeared not only signs of the crucifixion, but also other signs of the passion of Jesus. In fact, in answer to a precise question of Padre Agostino da San Marco in Lamis, the friar from Pietrelcina admitted that the Lord made him "experience […] his crowning with thorns and his flagellation," adding that such phenomena occurred over "many years […] and almost once a week."[36]

Finally, the future saint even bore the wound that Jesus himself received carrying the cross on his shoulder on the way to Calvary and he revealed its existence to a single human being: Father Karol Wojtyla.[37]

The Transverberation

In the letter in which Padre Pio told how the stigmata came about in San Giovanni Rotondo there is reference to "a mysterious figure, similar to the one seen on the evening of August 5th." Who was the individual who visited the priest a month and a half before the permanent impression of the wounds of Jesus on his body? And what happened on the evening of August 5th?

On the evening of August 5, 1918, while he was confessiong one of the boys from the seminary in his cell, no. 5 in the convent, Padre Pio was terrified by the "sight of a celestial figure" who appeared "before the eyes of his mind. He was holding a kind of tool, similar to a long iron blade with a well sharpened tip, and it seemed that flames came out of its point." Then the "figure" hurled the aforementioned tool "with all violence into his soul." With difficulty the Capuchin groaned. He felt that he was dying. He told the seminarian to leave because he didn't "have the strength to continue. This martyrdom lasted, without interruption, until the morning of the 7th."[38]

This is the mystical phenomenon known as transverberation, which consists of "a piercing of the epidermis and the penetration of a sharp object into the heart, be it by arrow, dart, or spear, through the work of God or of a heavenly creature of an angelic type. The transverberation is called a 'wound of love' when it manifests itself outwardly. It is also called an 'assault of the Seraphim' because this angel, with his intervention, inflames the heart with a burning love."[39] It is, in fact, an experience that scholars call "an exceptional communication of love due directly to the initiative and action of God […]. The strength and great power with which such communication is made, and at the same the depth it reaches within the human person, arouses in the soul the sensation of a stroke, of a wound that penetrates to the root of one's being, of one's powers, of one's consciousness."[40] And this radical perception "has the aim of preparing and disposing the person to that very deep and intimate union with God which mystics call 'transforming union,' where the soul becomes, through love and grace, one with God."[41]

The Other Gifts

To these major gifts, received by St. Pio of Pietrelcina, we must add at least some others among the most significant that characterized his earthly mission.

– **Xenoglossolia**, which is characteristic of those who "speak or write in a language normally unknown to them."[42]

Among the various episodes reported in several books on Padre Pio, we will include two written in his *Diary* by Padre Agostino da San Marco in Lamis:

"In 1940 or 41 a Swiss priest came to the Padre. He spoke in Latin with the Padre. Before he left, taking leave of Padre Pio, the priest recommended to his prayers a sick woman. The Padre replied in German: *Ich werde sie an die Göttliche Barmheizieheit empfehlen*: I am recommending her to Divine Mercy. The priest remained exceedingly impressed and full of wonder and he told this to the person who had put him up. Also in 1911, the Padre wrote to me - in response to a note of mine - a postcard in proper French, without any spelling errors."[43]

Padre Pio, however, knew neither German nor French,[44] and not even Greek.[45] For this the same Padre Agostino put his disciple to the test by writing to him in Aristotle's language. The result was the same, as Don Salvatore Pannullo testified at the bottom of that letter:

"Pietrelcina, August 25, 1919. I the undersigned certify here under the sanctity of the oath, that Padre Pio, after receiving this letter, literally explained to me its contents. Questioned by me how he could read and explain it, not even knowing the Greek alphabet, he replied: 'I know it! My Guardian Angel explained it all to me.'"[46]

– The scrutinizing of hearts (or discernment of spirits), which consists of the "supernatural knowledge of the secrets of God communicated to the heart,"[47]

In this regard the priest Vittorio Marcozzi, a Jesuit, in a study carried out as part of the cause for his beatification, wrote:

"Padre Pio enjoyed the gift of knowing consciences in a certain and infallible way, sometimes with regard to simple facts, sometimes of the most intimate secrets. Let us quote some facts, which prove that he knew facts regarding secrets of conscience [...].

He knows that Padre Agostino forgot the "Memento" during the Holy Mass, which he had been asked on the stairs by Padre Pio to remember. Padre Pio tells him so. […] He knows that a penitent had not been to confession for 25 years. He knows that two daughters had been prohibited by their dad who was a doctor to kiss the hands of Padre Pio, out of fear of tuberculosis. In the act of trying to kiss his hand, Padre Pio withdraws it, and says, 'No. Obey your father.' […] He knew the reason that Doctor Romanelli did not get a much hoped for grace, and, at the insistence of the doctor, he tells him the reason why: a serious failure that the doctor had forgotten."[48]

The same Padre Agostino noted, in his *Diary*, another episode:

"When Padre Pio was sick in Venafro in November 1911 one evening, before supper, I was advised that the Padre was ill and […] delirious […]. No one had noticed the preternatural and supernatural phenomena; neither had I; I thought he was actually seriously ill, indeed in danger of death. I ran to the room where there were other Friars and I saw the Padre lying in bed, with an agitated expression that said, 'Send away the cat who wants to hurl itself at me….' I could not take that scene and I went off to the choir to pray for the Padre, moaning out of fear that he was going to die. After more than a quarter of an hour I returned to the room and found Padre Pio alone, serene and joyful. As soon as he saw me he said: 'You went into the choir to pray, and you did well … you even thought of my eulogy … There is time, Padre, there's still time!'"[49]

This charism permitted the stigmatized Capuchin, in the performance of his ministry as a confessor, to awaken many deadened consciences and to allow the transforming action of divine mercy to renew the lifestyles of many penitents.[50]

– The radiation of light. Radiation refers to "the emission and/or the reflection of light from part of the human body."[51] Many have reported seeing the face of Padre Pio ablaze or transfigured. Dr. Giorgio Festa, a physician, on October 5, 1925 was working on the stigmatized Capuchin who had an inguinal hernia when he experienced this phenomenon. Taking advantage of the patient's collapse, he "furtively" took a look at the stigmata. From the outline of the double wound on the chest, "fresh and vermilion, in the form of a cross" (because there were actually two wounds: one of the transverberation and the second of the fifth wound of the crucifixion, that of the centurion's lance), there emanated "short, but visible rays of light."[52]

Padre Alberto D'Apolito, in addition to having "often" seen Padre Pio's face "bright or shining with indescribable beauty"[53], has collected and transcribed regarding this phenomenon the testimony of some witnesses, including the following:

> "In August of 1965 I accompanied Professor Guerini Rocco di Roma, a lover of the Franciscans and an admirer of Padre Pio, to Padre Pio's cell. [...] Upon leaving the room, Professor Guerini said to me: 'Padre Alberto, I am so happy. I looked at the face of Padre Pio; I thought it was the face of Jesus. It was so bright and beautiful, his two eyes shining like stars. Padre Pio is not a man of this world.'"[54]

– Bi-location, ie, the "presence of a person in two different places at the same moment."[55]

Apart from the two cases now known concerning Miss Giovanna Rizzani Boschi,[56] or the "visits" to the Cerase sisters of Foggia,[57] one could cite as an example the significant encounter that occurred with Cardinal József Mindszenty who "in October of 1956 was arrested, imprisoned and guarded. As time passed he expressed a very lively desire to be able to celebrate Mass. One morning Padre Pio presented him with everything he needed. The cardinal celebrated his holy Mass and Padre Pio served him; then they talked and eventually Padre Pio disappeared with what he had brought."[58] The incident was confirmed, albeit indirectly, by the protagonist of bilocations to Angelo Battisti, at the time director of the Casa Sollievo della Sofferenza and simultaneously employed by the Vatican Secretariat of State, who testified:

"A priest came from Budapest and, meeting me, he told me about this fact in confidence, begging me to obtain a confirmation of it from the Padre. [...] For over two to three years I never had an opportunity to ask the question. [...] If it had not happened that, one evening in March of 1965 (after so many years!), I finished asking the Padre regarding matters concerning the 'House,' and I got up to take my leave of him.

The Padre, in his goodness, instead invited me to stay a moment longer. I sat down again and without remotely thinking of Cardinal Mindszenty, I said to the Padre: 'Padre, did Cardinal Mindszenty recognize Padre Pio?'

He must have wanted to eat me alive, to treat me like an imbecile, someone stupid. But when he told me and explained that he had been reading my thoughts, that it was not my intention to bother him on this topic, that I did not do so out of curiosity, but that God, for his glory at that time put this on my lips, the Padre became good and he replied: 'So What! We met and we talked. Do you wish that he had not recognized me?'

Then he became sad and added: 'The devil is ugly, but they have made me uglier than the devil' [...]. The Padre concluded: 'Remember to pray for this great confessor of the faith, who has suffered so much for the Church.'"[59]

– **Osmogenesis** "consists in the issuance of an intense fragrance from a person's body."[60]

Many perceived this with respect to Padre Pio both during his lifetime and after his death. "His presence could be detected through an extraordinary variety and intensity of odors with different shades: greenhouse smells, carbolic acid, roses, lilies, jasmine, incense, the finest tobacco and others."[61] Even Padre Agostino da San Marco in Lamis, whose olfactory buds[62] had atrophied, was aware of this.

The aroma emanated primarily from the blood of the stigmatized Capuchin, as Dr. Giorgio Festa was able to ascertain. He certified:

"The blood that flows in drops from the wounds that Padre Pio has on his person possesses a fine and delicate fragrance that many of those who approach him have had the opportunity to experience distinctly. Regarding this phenomenon I said nothing at the time of my first encounter with him[63] since, being devoid of any sense of smell, I was not in a position to express any personal judgment regarding it [...].

Padre Pio does not, nor has he ever used any kind of perfume: However, many of those who have approached him assert that a pleasant scent almost a mixture of violets and roses emanates from his person. [...] As for me, I can say that in my first visit

I took from his side a linen cloth soaked in blood, which I brought with me for a microscopic investigation. For the reason already mentioned, I did not personally experience any special emanation from it: however, a distinguished official and other persons who returned from San Giovanni Rotondo in the car with me, without knowing that I had locked that linen cloth kept in a box I had brought with me, despite the intense ventilation caused by the speed of the running vehicle, they sensed the fragrance very strongly, and assured me that it responded specifically to the scent that emanates from the person of Padre Pio.

Once in Rome, during the following days and for a long period of time thereafter, the same linen cloth, kept in a cabinet in my office, perfumed the environment so thoroughly that many of the people who came to consult me spontaneously asked about its origin."[64]

But "this mysterious aroma was perceived both by those who were close to the venerated Padre and those who were at a distance from him," even "at hundreds of kilometers away, even from overseas, usually in circumstances related to the person of Padre Pio." On one occasion a spiritual daughter asked him the meaning of that particular odor. The future saint replied, "It just indicates my presence."[65]

– **Ecstasies**, "the departure of the human being, body and soul, from the confines of itself, becoming alien and estranged from the self. In such a condition the individual transfers into God all his intellectual, volitional and sensitive faculties losing all sensability, self control and real relationship with the outside world. This experience of the divine is strong enough as to involve both the body and the soul. The ecstatic person, although not seeing or feeling anything, is not asleep. […] He or she is flooded with unspeakable joy and is, by divine grace, placed in the state of an experience of communion with the Lord that can only be defined as ineffable and especially profound."[66]

Those that Padre Pio experienced in the convent of Venafro, Isernia, were noted by Padre Agostino da San Marco in Lamis in some notebooks published under the title *Diary* in which we read:

> "The ecstasies were almost continuous: they took place two or three times a day and lasted from one to two hours at a time. In that of [Nov] 29-11 and that of [Dec] 3-12 a doctor was present."[67]

The doctor referred to by Padre Agostino is Dr. Nicola Lombardi of Pozzilli, a town near Venafro, who certified:

> "Padre Pio […] was lying on the bed with his eyes open, his face red, his eyes fixed on something as if it were in front of him; he spoke to Christ, the Virgin Mary and Guardian Angel. The dialogue or soliloquy that he carried on was not disconnected. This lasted about half an hour in my presence and in that of the friars. During this state I saw that his heart, pulse, and everything was physiological.
>
> After the dialogue, because the characters with whom he had made it withdrew, he closed his eyes and fell asleep. If the guardian, in this state of sleep, had called him from outside the cell not allowing him to hear his voice as he did in my presence, he would wake up laughing and joking as if nothing had ever happened.
>
> During the period of dialogue, he was not aware of anything around him. […] I judged that Padre Pio was taken up in a form of ecstasy."[68]

– **Visions**, which are "private revelations, that is, divine messages that God gives to the human heart enabling it to perceive objects naturally invisible to man. The word *vision* properly speaking refers to the sense of sight; however, especially in the mystical sphere, it has a broader meaning that extends from analyzing to understanding."[69] Padre Pio started experiencing these at an early age. Padre Agostino writes in his *Diary* that "the apparitions began in his fifth year of age, when he had the thought and desire to consecrate himself forever to the Lord, and they were continuing."[70] But little Francesco Forgione never in the world thought that he was living a supernatural experience and held the belief, even after his priestly ordination, that they were occurrences common to every human being. Indeed, Padre Agostino's notes continue:

> "Asked why he had hidden them for so long a time[71] he candidly replied that he did not manifest them for he believed that they were ordinary things that all souls would experience; in fact, one day he said naively: 'And do you not see the Madonna?' To my negative response he added: 'You say that out of holy humility!'"[72]

Responding to the request for more clarification, asked of him by his spiritual director, Padre Benedetto da San Marco in Lamis[73], Padre Pio tried to describe what it is not easy to translate into human words:

> "The events that the Lord reveals to my soul are to be distinguished as well: in manifestations and purely supernatural apparitions, those regarding beings without form, and manifestations of those having human forms.
> The first have to do with God, his perfections, his attributes. These

I can't in any way put into writing notwithstanding the fact that they are present in my mind, as this paper on which I am writing is present. […] As to the other kinds of manifestation they have to do with our Lord as a human figure; at the Last Supper, in the garden dripping blood, bound to the column, glorious and resplendent in his resurrection and in other ways. Still others regard the Queen of the Angels and other heavenly personages clothed with human forms. Of these things the soul somehow manages to express itself, but would prefer to withdraw into perfect silence, because to see the distance that exists between the thing seen and the great distance that exists between it and what one tries to express is painful."[74]

Often celestial visions followed diabolical harassment. Padre Pio revealed to Padre Agostino:

"*Barbablu*[75] [Bluebeard] does not want to surrender. He took almost all forms. For several days he came to visit me here along with his other satellites armed with sticks and iron weapons and what is worse in their own forms.

Who knows how many times he has thrown me out of bed and dragged me around the room. But patience! Jesus, our heavenly Mother, the Angel, St. Joseph and our Padre St. Francis are almost always with me."[76]

And then he added that these "celestial figures with their frequent visits," reinforced what he suffered from the demon.[77]

– **Clairvoyance**, that is, "the faculty that allows you to see with the intellect things not perceptible through the mediation of the senses or to predict the future development of things.

It is about seeing things hidden, or listening at a considerable distance or predicting the future without the usual cooperation of the senses."[78]

Sometimes God allowed Padre Pio to disclose events that could not have been known in any way by human means. It happened many times, during the two World Wars, with the relatives of the soldiers who asked for news about their loved ones at the front and it also happened in some particular circumstances.

The first involved the sending to San Giovanni Rotondo, by Benedict XV, of Padre Luigi Besi, postulator of the Passionists, who reached Foggia at the same time as Prof. Raffaele Battistini, the personal physician of the Pope.[79] Their journey had to be secret. But Padre Pio, shortly before their arrival, said to his Guardian: "Send the convent car to the station, because a Passionist religious, sent personally by the Holy Father, is coming."[80] Battistini, when he saw the unexpected and inexplicable automobile of the friars, thought that he no longer needed to meet the friar, but to return immediately to Rome to report to His Holiness what had happened."[81] Besi, however, completed his task.

Two other incidents had to do with Pope Pius XII: the Capuchin of Pietrelcina not only saw him in Paradise immediately after his death, but he showed himself aware of the existence of a plan to kidnap the Pope, put together by Adolf Hitler which Hitler had communicated only to Heinrich Himmler his right-hand man and to the one who was supposed to perform the task, General Karl Wolff. Also he was able to know that this proposal had been foiled. At that same moment, in fact, while he was in the choir of the old church of the convent of San Giovanni Rotondo, Padre Pio told the former mayor of the town, Francesco Morcaldi[82] "Ciccillo, the Pope will be saved!"[83]

The Sense of the Charisms

God, therefore, has given many and extraordinary gifts to one man, Padre Pio of Pietrelcina. At this point only those who do not know or have not read carefully or do not want to read the testimonies and documents surrounding the cause of beatification and canonization, now largely published, have doubts about this.

Are all these extraordinary gifts sufficient to declare the sanctity of the humble friar from Pietrelcina?

Absolutely not. In fact all that has been exposed so far has nothing to do with holiness. Or at most it has very little.

The *Catechism of the Catholic Church*, in fact, referring to the Conciliar Constitution *Lumen Gentium*, teaches us that these "special graces" [called "charisms"] have the sole function of "making the faithful suitable and ready to undertake various tasks and offices useful in the renewal of the Church and in the development of its constitution."[84] Therefore they are aimed at the "building of the Church for the good of men and the needs of the world"[85], but on condition that "they are gifts that truly come from the Holy Spirit and are exercised in full conformity with the authentic impulses of the same Spirit, that is in keeping with charity, the true measure of all charisms."[86] Even the devil can perform miracles. And also because some, although privileged with divine gifts, mount them with pride and, without even realizing it, are dragged by the leash of vanity into the enemy's net. But this never happened to Padre Pio, who always walked the road of humility. Three may be enough, among the countless episodes testified to by various witnesses, to get an idea.

Padre Eusebio Notte said:

"I didn't know how to explain why people come to him. More than once he confided to me: 'What are these people doing here?' In other circumstances, he added: 'If they could only guess who I am, they would flee.'"[87]

Padre Carmelo Durante wrote:

"For a soul who asked for prayers to get a grace […] and turned to the Padre, saying: 'Padre, you are so good …' He replied abruptly: 'I am not good; only Jesus is good. I do not know how this habit of St. Francis that I wear does not run away from me! The last delinquent in the land is like gold compared to me.'"[88]

These might seem to be exaggerated expressions, but they actually reveal Padre Pio's particular awareness of sin, understood as a lack of correspondence to the love of God. In fact, Fra Marcellino Iasenzaniro explains it this way:

"His concern was that he would not render unto the Lord in proportion to his divine munificence, who had enriched him with so many gifts. […] Dramatically illumined by grace, the more he grew in the knowledge of the greatness and goodness of God, the more he discovered the depths of his misery that separated him from him."[89]

The same Fra Marcellino transcribed another significant testimony regarding the humility of his holy confrere:

"One summer evening in 1958, during the recreation that Padre Pio granted himself along with his confreres and spiritual sons after Sunday Mass, a young priest said: 'Padre, you are for us like a faucet through which pass the answers to all our apprehensions, concerns, desires, etc….'

Padre Pio stiffened up and exclaimed: 'Young man, did you come here to tempt me?'

Then, softening a bit, he added: 'Your expression may be right as long as you recognize that the faucet would be a useless tool, if there was not the water of grace which flows through it.'"[90]

In any case there is no necessary link between the manifestation of extraordinary gifts and holiness. The charisms are "oriented toward sanctifying grace"[91], that is they are granted to collect the fruits of holiness. This same Padre Pio was so convinced of this that to a spiritual daughter he said,

"Look, these gifts, like the reading of hearts, clairvoyance, the spirit of prophecy, etc. the Lord gives them to souls not for their personal sanctification, but because they appeal to other souls and draw them to him. All these things do not increase sanctifying grace, but are means to call other souls to God."[92]

But God can use anyone to do anything to intervene in an extraordinary way in human history in order to draw every man to his fundamental vocation, which is to become a saint. Therefore "the miracles of Christ and the saints, prophecies … are the most certain signs of Divine Revelation. Adapted to the understanding of all, they are motives of credibility which show that the assent of faith is not a blind reminder of the spirit."[93] So the signs are for us, who are so many doubting

Thomases, to support our weak faith. They do not serve the saints. And they do not serve to make saints.

Charity is another essential requirement. "Charity is the soul of the holiness to which all are called."[94]

Pope Emeritus Benedict XVI, citing the first letter of John, at the beginning of his encyclical *Deus Caritas Est* reminded us that: "God is love; whoever remains in love remains in God and God in him. By creating man in his image and likeness God crowned him with glory (i.e., gave him a share in his holiness), but man, by sinning, was deprived of the Glory of God," as the *Catechism of the Church* continues to proclaim.[95] What does all this mean? When we read in Genesis that "God created man in his own image"[96] it does not mean that the Eternal Father has the eyes, nose, long white hair and bushy white beard as shown in bold images of the Blessed Trinity. Beyond the metaphor it does not mean that God's thoughts are to coincide with my thoughts, that his will must adapt itself to mine, that I can remember him and use him only when I need to solve a problem for which the "recommendations" of the "powerful" of the earth have proved ineffective. That is a God "created" in the image of man. John's concept of God, rather, is a love in which we understand man's likeness with God, which consists precisely in the ability to love. And we will resemble him the more we love, that is the more God himself and other men are loved, because "love of God and love of one's neighbor are inseparable."[97] Padre Pio himself said: "Love is nothing but the spark of God in men."[98] That's why "only in the mystery of the Incarnate Word does the mystery of man take on light." In fact, Jesus has loved man unto the ultimate sacrifice: "The innocent Lamb, with his blood poured out freely has earned us life; in him God has reconciled us to himself and to one another." In this way "the image of the invisible God" (Col 1:15) has come to our eyes" and "the perfect man has restored to the children of Adam that likeness to God, which suffered deformation early on because of sin."[99] He is, therefore, the way to holiness.

The Capuchin of Pietrelcina is holy because, following in the footsteps of Christ as an authentic son of St. Francis he "has exercised in a heroic degree the theological virtues of faith, hope and charity, both towards God and towards our neighbor, and the cardinal virtues of prudence, justice, fortitude, temperance, and associated virtues." He is holy because, "inflamed by the love of God and love of neighbor, Padre Pio lived to the full his vocation to work for the redemption of man, according to the special mission which marked all his life. He put this program into effect by three means: through the direction of souls, through sacramental reconciliation of sinners, and through the celebration of the Holy Mass."[100] Thus the Congregation for the Causes of Saints spoke, revealing a shocking truth that when the Capuchin of Pietrelcina was still alive, Padre Benedetto da San Marco in Lamis alone had intuited.[101]

But what does it mean that "Padre Pio lived to the full his vocation to work for the redemption of man"?

For a complete answer to this question we must first remember what the holy Capuchin had inscribed on the holy card for his priestly ordination: "*With You* I am for the world / Way, Truth, Life / *And for You* Holy Priest / Perfect Victim."[102] Those beautiful words were not just for the occasion. They can be understood only by reading a letter written by the same Capuchin a few months later, November 29, 1910, to the same Padre Benedetto:

"And so I come now, my Padre, to ask your permission. For some time I have felt in me a need, that is, to offer myself to the Lord as a victim for sinners and for the souls in purgatory. This desire has been growing more and more in my heart so much so that it has now become, I would say, a strong passion."

But, once having asked permission, a few lines later he confessed to his spiritual director:

"It is true that I made this offering to the Lord several times, begging him to want to pour over me the punishments that are prepared for sinners and the souls in purgatory even multiplying them a hundred fold over me, as long as sinners are converted and saved and the souls in purgatory are admitted quickly into paradise, but now I want to make this offering to the Lord under the vow of obedience."[103]

His spiritual director gave his approval. "Feel free to make the offering of which you speak…," he said, adding, "which will be most acceptable to the Lord." And then he encouraged him,

"Stretch out your arms on your cross offering to the Father the sacrifice of yourself in union with the tender Savior, suffer, moan and pray for the lawless of the land and for the wretched of the Hereafter."[104]

When he wrote these words, Padre Benedetto did not know, as we wrote earlier, that the Lord had already accepted this offer and had sealed this pact of total love with the marks of his wounds (the first stigmata).

Here, then, is why Padre Pio is a saint. Because he so loved God and humanity as to ask and to accept, day after day, a long life of suffering (not only the physical wounds and illnesses, but also the humiliation, deprivation, slander, loneliness and spiritual aridity) in order to save sinners, living or dead, and to share, for this purpose, the cross of Christ. So all his extraordinary gifts did not serve to make him a saint, but to make his faith exemplary[105] and to give credibility to his mission, which was to help others become saints. They were the instruments through which God's mercy has attracted men to renew, once again, with them his covenant of love. As Padre Fердınаndo da Riese Pio X in his biography *Padre Pio da Pietrelcina: crocifisso senza croce* [Padre Pio of Pietrelcina: crucified without the cross]:

"To make the conversion of the world to God more attractive and obligatory, to make the man sent by God more visible and identifiable for this purpose, the same Sender enriched the mandate with gifts. They were extraordinary and terrible at the same time. Found in Padre Pio, they had to be for him the same credentials to show, for the other reasons to believe. They had to be the monstrance of his saving mission. Once again, in the history of salvation, God resorted to signs, to help men believe. He placed under the eyes of men proofs, such as to cause men to surrender confronted with the evidence. Men must know how to collect and read the signs. First, the most obvious signs such as the stigmata, the scents, bilocation, the reading of consciences."[106]

This is one opinion, also shared by two influential pastors of the Church of the last century: Cardinal Giuseppe Siri, archbishop of Genoa, who believed the charisms of Padre Pio to be "motives of credibility" conferred by God on this sought after confessor "for his mission"[107], and Cardinal Corrado

Ursi, archbishop of Naples, according to whom:

"the miracles, bilocation, discernment of spirits and prophecies [...] what was their purpose? [...] These wonderful things he has accomplished as an instrument of Divine Love, have been providential means to accredit the ministry of reconciliation with God, which he suffered to the point of immolation in order to attract many, many sinners, especially inveterate ones, the hardened, and the impervious to every other ray of divine grace, to the washing of the spirit, the revival in God, the reconquest of the supreme freedom of God's children."[108]

Notes for Chapter II

1. Cf. A. Bobbio, A. Tradigo, "I santi nella storia. I più amati dagli italiani", in *Famiglia Cristiana*, n. 45, del 5 novembre 2006, pp. 66 e ss.
2. "Informatio super dubio" in *Beatificationis et Canonizationis Ven. Servi Dei Pii in Pietrelcina. Positio super miraculo*, Tipografia Guerra, Rome 1998, p. 4.
3. Cf. p. 5.
4. Cf. pp. 16 et seq.
5. Cf. p. 21.
6. Cf. "Report on the session of the Medical Commission of the Congregation for the Causes of Saints," in *Positio super miraculo*, op. cit., 1998, p. 6.
7. Cf. G. Di Flumeri, *Il Beato Padre Pio da Pietrelcina*, Edizioni Padre Pio da Pietrelcina, San Giovanni Rotondo (FG) 2001, pp. 305 et seq.
8. Cf. "Chronological Case in point," in *Canonizationis da Beato Pii a Pietrelcina. Positio super miraculo*, Tipografia Guerra, Rome 2001, pp. 2 et seq.
9. "Informatio super dubio" in *Positio super miraculo*, op. cit., 2001, p. 3.
10. "Nella casistica della letteratura internazionale viene riportata una mortalità del 100%, quando gli organi interessati ed insufficienti sono

superiori a 5" ("Fattispecie cronologica," in *Positio super miraculo,* op. cit., 2001, p. 35).

11. Cf. pp. 7-8.
12. "Informatio super dubio," in ibid, p. 8.
13. "Chronological Case in point" in ibid, pp. 9-10.
14. Cf. "Informatio super dubio," in ibid, pp. 12 et seq.
15. Cf. "Chronological Case in point," in ibid, p. 8.
16. Cf. pp. 12 et seq.
17. Ibid, pp. 29-30.
18. Cf. "Report on the session of the Medical Commission of the Congregation for the Causes of Saints," in ibid, p. 7.
19. Congregation for the Causes of Saints, "Decree on the miracle," in *Voce di Padre Pio,* year XXXIII, n. 4, April 2002, p. 27.
20. "Letter of Padre Pio to Padre Benedetto da San Marco in Lamis of 22 October 1918", in P. Pietrelcina, *Letters,* M. Pobladura, A. Ripabottoni (Ed.), Edizioni Padre Pio da Pietrelcina, San Giovanni Rotondo (FG) 1995, vol. I, p. 1093.
21. F. Castelli, *Padre Pio sotto inchiesta. L'"autobiografia" segreta,* Edizioni Ares, Milano 2008, p. 220.
22. "From the medical point of view the stigmata can be defined as skin lesions or signs of blood, of varying shape, depth and location that bleed with varying extent and frequency (usually on Fridays or during liturgical celebrations that recall the Passion of Jesus). These 'wounds' and / or bleeding episodes occur spontaneously, i.e., without any apparent traumatic cause [...]. Their main characteristic is to form a syndrome that immediately recalls the martyrdom of Jesus to which he was subjected during his Passion in the period from his bloody sweat in the Garden of Olives to his death by crucifixion, which was confirmed by the spear of a Roman soldier. The following phenomena, therefore, fall within the definition of *stigmata passionis*: the bloody sweat (or hematohydrosis) (cf. Lk 22:44), the wounds caused by the crown of thorns and the scourging (cf. Mk 15:17; Jn 19:1), injuries caused by beatings, by the weight of the cross and falls during the climb to Calvary (cf. Mt 26:67; Mk 14:65; Jn 18:22), the continuity of skin and muscle-tendon, localized to the hands (anatomically designed as carpal, metacarpal and fingers) and feet produced by the true crucifixion with nails and the penetrating wound at the base of the lung caused by the spear of one of the soldiers confirming death (cf. Jn 19:33-34) (P.M. Marianeschi,

"Stimmate", in L. Borriello, R. Di Muro (Ed.), *Dizionario dei fenomeni mistici cristiani*, Àncora, Milano 2014, pp. 128-129).

23. Maria Anna (Mariannina), called Nina, Campanile was the fourth of ten children of Nicola and Maria Formica, both of San Giovanni Rotondo. Along with some of her sisters, Nina attended high school and earned a master's degree; taught in primary schools in San Giovanni Rotondo. The first call of the mother and older sister to go up to the convent with them to see the "holy friar", who had arrived a few days earlier, Nina responded with a flat refusal. A tragic family event made her go to the convent sooner than she thought: On September 16, 1916 her younger brother Pasqualino died at the front and her mother, after prayers and Masses, anxious regarding the eternal fate of her son, ordered Nina to go to ask the "holy friar" if her brother was safe. On October 5, accompanied by the teacher Victorina Ventrella, she saw Padre Pio for the first time, and having asked him, she heard the answer: "If God's mercy should weigh as heavily as you think, all men would go to hell. He is saved, yes, and he needs suffrages." This first meeting would be followed by many others, from which arose a long and unbroken spiritual direction, both verbal and epistolary, when events forced the one or the other to be away from San Giovanni Rotondo.

24. "Testimonianza di Nina Campanile", in G. Di Flumeri (Ed.), *Le stigmate di Padre Pio da Pietrelcina*, Edizioni Padre Pio da Pietrelcina, San Giovanni Rotondo (FG) 1985, pp. 140-141.

25. "Testimonianza di Vittoria Ventrella", in G. Di Flumeri (Ed.), *Le stigmate di Padre Pio da Pietrelcina*, op. cit., pp. 141-142.

26. P. da Casacalenda, *Le mie memorie intorno a Padre Pio*, Edizioni Padre Pio da Pietrelcina, San Giovanni Rotondo (FG) 1978, pp. 111 e ss.

27. "Letter of Padre Pio to Padre Benedetto of October 17, 1918," in *Epistolario*, op. cit., vol. I, p. 1090.

28. "Letter of Padre Pio to Padre Benedetto of October 19, 1918," in *Epistolario*, op. cit., vol. I, p. 1091.

29. Cf. supra.

30. "Letter of Padre Pio to Padre Benedetto of October 22, 1918," in *Epistolario*, op. cit., vol. I, p. 1093.

31. "Letter of Padre Pio to Padre Agostino of October 10, 1915," in *Epistolario*, op. cit., vol. I, p. 669.

32. "Letter of Padre Pio to Padre Benedetto of September 8, 1911," in *Epistolario*, op. cit., vol. I, p. 234.

33. P.M. Marianeschi, "La scomparsa delle stimmate di Padre Pio", in *Atti del Convegno di studio sulle stimmate del Servo di Dio Padre Pio da Pietrelcina*, Edizioni Padre Pio da Pietrelcina, San Giovanni Rotondo (FG) 1988, p. 245.

34. It took place at San Giovanni Rotondo from September 16 to 20, 1987.

35. P. M. Marianeschi, "La scomparsa delle stimmate di Padre Pio", in *Atti del Convegno di studio sulle stimmate*, op. cit., pp. 238 e ss.

36. Cf. "Letter of Padre Pio to Padre Agostino of October 10, 1915," in *Collected Letters*, op. cit., Vol. I, p. 669.

37. Cf. S. Campanella, *Il Papa e il Frate*, Edizioni Padre Pio da Pietrelcina, San Giovanni Rotondo (FG) 2007, p. 53 e ss.; cf. also M. da Pietrelcina, *Io... testimone del Padre*, Edizioni Padre Pio da Pietrelcina, San Giovanni Rotondo (FG) 2013, pp. 155 e ss.

38. Cf. "Letter of Padre Pio to Padre Benedetto of August 21, 1918," in *Epistolario*, op. cit., vol. I, p. 1065.

39. R. Di Muro, "Transverberazione," in L. Borriello, R. Di Muro (Ed.), *Dizionario dei fenomeni mistici cristiani*, op. cit., p. 138.

40. R. Moretti, "La transverberazione di Padre Pio," in *Atti del Convegno di studio sulle stimmate*, op. cit., p. 314.

41. Ibid, p. 309.

42. Istituto della Enciclopedia Italiana fondata da Giovanni Treccani, *Enciclopedia Italiana*, vol. XXXV, p. 820.

43. A. da San Marco in Lamis, *Diario*, Edizioni Padre Pio da Pietrelcina, San Giovanni Rotondo (FG) 2012, p. 181.

44. Cf. ibid.

45. Cf. ibid, p. 288.

46. P. da Pietrecina, *Epistolario*, op. cit., vol. I, p. 302, n. 2.

47. F. Armenti, "Discernimento degli spiriti," in L. Borriello, R. Di Muro (Ed.), *Dizionario dei fenomeni mistici cristiani*, op. cit., p. 46.

48. V. Marcozzi, "Considerazioni sui fatti straordinari di Padre Pio", in *Positio super virtutibus*, op. cit., vol. IV, parte III, p. 256.

49. A. da San Marco in Lamis, *Diario*, op. cit., pp. 288-289.

50. Cf. chapter 1.

51. P.M. Marianeschi, "Irradiazione luminosa," in L. Borriello, R. Di Muro (Ed.), *Dizionario dei fenomeni mistici cristiani*, p. 76.

52. Cf. G. Festa, *Misteri di scienza e luci di fede. Le stigmate del Padre Pio da Pietrelcina*, Stabilimento Tipolitografico Vittorio Ferri, Roma 1938², p. 215.

53. Cf. A. D'Apolito, *Padre Pio da Pietrelcina. Ricordi, esperienze, testimonianze*, Edizioni Padre Pio da Pietrelcina, San Giovanni Rotondo (FG) 1978, p. 94.

54. Ibid, p. 97.

55. F. Armenti, "Bilocazione," in L. Borriello, R. Di Muro (Ed.), *Dizionario dei fenomeni mistici cristiani*, op. cit., p. 29. Cf. also ibid, pp. 174 e ss.

56. Cf. P. da Pietrelcina, *Epistolario*, op. cit., vol. IV, p. 1029; "Testimonianza di Giovanna Rizzani ved. Boschi", in *Positio super virtutibus*, op. cit., vol. II, p. 109 e s.

57. Cf. P. da Pietrelcina, *Epistolario*, op. cit., vol. II, pp. 185, 208 e 258.

58. Cf. "Testimonianza di Angelo Battisti", in *Positio super virtutibus*, op. cit., vol. II, p. 1638.

59. Ibid, pp. 1638-1639.

60. F. Armenti, "Osmogenesi", in L. Borriello, R. Di Muro (Ed.), *Dizionario dei fenomeni mistici cristiani*, op. cit., p. 103.

61. G. Preziuso, "Padre Pio: un Santo ricco di carismi (8). Il dono del profumo", in *Voce di Padre Pio*, anno XXXVII, n. 2, febbraio 2006, p. 40.

62. Cf. A. da San Marco in Lamis, *Diario*, op. cit., p. 179.

63. Dr. Giorgio Festa visited Padre Pio, as a representative of the Minister General of the Capuchins, the first time in October of 1919 and the second time a year later along with Dr. Luigi Romanelli.

64. G. Festa, *Misteri di scienza e luci di fede*, op. cit., pp. 152-153.

65. Cf. G. Preziuso, "Padre Pio, a saint full of gifts (8). The gift of perfume," in *Voice of Padre Pio*, February 2006, pp. 41-42. The journalist Giovanni Gigliozzi and his wife noticed the perfume of Padre Pio even in the stairs which normally had the "dirty and smelly" odor of a post office (Cf. G. Gigliozzi, ... *And Padre Pio said to me* ..., Newton & Compton, Rome 2001, p. 65).

66. R. Di Muro, 'Ecstasy', in L. Borriello, R. Di Muro (Ed.), *Dictionary of Christian mystical phenomena*, op. cit., p. 54.

67. A. da San Marco in Lamis, *Diario*, op. cit., p. 49.

68. "Letter of Dr. Nicola Lombardi to Padre Agostino of February 13, 1912," in *Voice of Padre Pio*, year IV, no. 3, March 1973, p. 7.

69. R. Talmelli, "Visions," in L. Borriello, R. Di Muro (Ed.), *Dictionary of Christian mystical phenomena*, op. cit., p. 144.

70. Cf. A. da San Marco in Lamis, *Diario*, op. cit., p. 53.

71. Until 1915, when Padre Agostino wrote this note.

72. A. da San Marco in Lamis, *Diario*, op. cit., p. 53.

73. Cf. "Letter of Padre Benedetto to Padre Pio of 15 January, 1913," in *Collected Letters*, op. cit., Vol. I, p. 371.

74. "Letter of Padre Pio to Padre Benedetto of June 20, 1913," in *Collected Letters*, op. cit., Vol. I, pp. 373 et seq.
75. It is one of the names by which Padre Pio called the devil.
76. "Letter of Padre Pio to Padre Agostino of January 18, 1912," in *Collected Letters*, op. cit., Vol. I, p. 252.
77. Cf. "Letter of Padre Pio to Padre Agostino of January 1912," in *Collected Letters*, op. cit., Vol. I, p. 255.
78. R. Di Muro, 'Clairvoyance', in L. Borriello, R. Di Muro (Ed.), *Dictionary of Christian mystical phenomena*, op. cit., p. 34.
79. Cf. *Positio super virtutibus*, op. cit., Vol. IV, p. 50; Padre Pio of Pietrelcina, *Letters*, op. cit., Vol. I, p. 14; G. Saldutto, *A tormented seven years in the life of Padre Pio of Pietrelcina*, Pontificia Universitas Gregoriana, Rome, 1974, p. 140. These sources report, however, the name of Dr. Bastianelli. More precisely in the records of the trial the name of Professor Giuseppe Bastianelli is cited (Cf. *Positio super virtutibus*, op. cit., vol. IV, p. 50 and *Beatificationis et Canonizationis Servi Dei Pii in Pietrelcina. Positio super virtutibus*, vol. I / 1, Tipolitografia Signum, Bollate (MI) 1997, p. 409, n. 34), stating that he was the "personal physician of Pope Benedict XV." In fact the Pope's personal doctor was Prof. Raffaele Battistini (Cf. *Annuario Pontificio*, 1918, p. 596). Only *A tormented seven years,* however, cites the dual source of information: an article published by *Eco of Saint Gabriel* in August 1973, pages 236-237, entitled "Providential Encounters" and signed by Padre Filippo d'Amando and the first volume of *Letters of Padre Pio*, p. 14. Since the latter contains the name of Bastianelli from the time of its first edition (1971) it is likely to be the source of this error.
80. *Positio super virtutibus*, op. cit., Vol. IV, p. 50.
81. F. Spaccucci, *The five popes of Padre Pio*, Laurentian, Napoli 1968, p. 37.
82. He was born in San Giovanni Rotondo on November 2, 1889; for three terms he was mayor of his city (1923-1927, 1954-1959 and 1962-1965). Steady, sincere and devoted friend of Padre Pio and his confreres he died August 18, 1976.
83. Cf. S. Campanella, "Pius XII. The Pope that Padre Pio 'saw' in Paradise", in *Studies on Padre Pio*, year VIII, no. 3, September-December 2007, pp. 499 et seq.
84. Cf. *Catechism of the Catholic Church*, 798.
85. Cf. ibid, 799.
86. Ibid, 800.
87. "Testimony of Padre Eusebio Notte," in *Positio super virtutibus*, op. cit., Vol. II, p. 301.

88. C. Sessano, *Testimony of Padre Pio*, op. cit., p. 7.
89. M. Iasenzaniro, *Padre Pio. Profile of a saint*, Edizioni Padre Pio da Pietrelcina, vol. I, San Giovanni Rotondo (FG) 2009, pp. 255 et seq.
90. Ibid, pp. 268-269.
91. Cf. *Catechism of the Catholic Church*, 2003.
92. G. Preziuso, "Padre Pio, a saint full of gifts (8). The gift of fragrance," in *Voce di Padre Pio*, February 2006, p. 40.
93. *Catechism of the Catholic Church*, 156.
94. Ibid, 826.
95. Ibid, 2809.
96. Gen 1:27.
97. Benedict XVI, *Deus Caritas Est*, encyclical letter on Christian love, December 25, 2005, 18.
98. G. Leone, *Padre Pio e la sua Opera*, Edizioni Casa Sollievo della Sofferenza, San Giovanni Rotondo (FG) 2006, p. 48.
99. Cf. *Gaudium et Spes, the Pastoral Constitution on the Church in the Modern World*, December 7, 1965, 22. The same conciliar document explains that "whoever follows Christ, the perfect man, becomes himself more of a man" (*Gaudium et Spes*, 41).
100. Congregation for the Causes of Saints, "Decreto sulle virtú," December 18, 1997, in *Voce di Padre Pio*, year XXIX, n. 6, June 1998 pp. 26 et seq.
101. He himself explained that he had received a "vocation to co-redeem." Cf. "Letter of Padre Benedetto to Padre Pio of August 27, 1918," in *Collected Letters*, op. cit., Vol. I, p. 1068.
102. F. da Riese Pio X, *Padre Pio, crocifisso senza croce*, Edizioni Padre Pio, San Giovanni Rotondo (FG) 2007, p. 85.
103. "Letter of Padre Pio to Padre Benedetto of November 29, 1910," in *Collected Letters*, op. cit., Vol. I, p. 206.
104. "Letter of Padre Benedetto to Padre Pio of December 1, 1910," in *Collected Letters*, op. cit., Vol. I, p. 207.
105. Cf. Mk 16:17 to 18.
106. F. da Riese Pio X, *Padre Pio, crocifisso senza croce*, op. cit., p. 206.
107. Cf. G. Preziuso, "Padre Pio, a saint full of gifts (9). The gift of prophecy," in *Voce di Padre Pio*, thirty-seventh year, n. 3, March 2006, p. 31.
108. C. Ursi, "The message of Padre Pio," spoken before of the monumental *Via Crucis* blessing speech in San Giovanni Rotondo, May 25, 1971, in *Voce di Padre Pio*, year II, no. 7-8, July-August, 1971, p. 4.

Chapter III

MERCIFUL PADRE PIO

Padre Pio did not limit himself to dispensing the mercy of the Lord through the sacrament of Reconciliation, but was a concrete and direct witness of the mercy announced by Jesus through his life and through the Word:

> "You have heard that it was said, 'An eye for an eye and a tooth for a tooth.' But I say to you, offer no resistance to one who is evil. When someone strikes you on your right cheek, turn the other side to him as well. If anyone wants to go to law with you over your tunic, hand him your cloak as well. Should anyone press you into service for one mile, go with him for two miles. Give to the one who asks of you, and do not turn your back on one who wants to borrow."
>
> "You have heard that it was said, 'You shall love your neighbor and hate your enemy.' But I say to you, love your enemies, and pray for those who persecute you, that you may be children of your heavenly Father, for he makes his sun rise on the bad and the good, and causes rain to fall on the just and the unjust. For if you love those who love

you, what recompense will you have? Do not the tax collectors do the same? And if you greet your brothers only, what is unusual with that? Do not the pagans do the same?"[1]

Having committed himself, temporarily on January 22, 1904 and permanently on January 27, 1907, to "observe the holy Gospel of our Lord Jesus Christ by living in obedience, without anything of his own and in chastity,"[2] according to the Rule of Saint Francis, and the Constitutions of the Capuchin Friars Minor, the religious of Pietrelcina followed the teaching and example of the Son of God even in the most difficult situations of his long and tormented existence, to which the four stories of pardon mentioned in the present chapter refer.

Don Giovanni Miscio

At the beginning "of December 1925 Miss Maria Pompilio, an elementary school teacher," during a conversation with a "teaching colleague," canon Don Giovanni Miscio, learned that the priest had written "a brochure"[3] that he was preparing to have printed, containing some "offensive insinuations" about Padre Pio, who was described as "a strange and sometimes subconscious blind instrument in the hands of some of the friars greedy for the gain they could derive from the offerings of his devotees; at other times he is described as a proud person with a certain vain attitude of superiority toward the other Ministers of the Church, and would voluntarily isolate himself with a small circle of zealous women, and finally at other times, involve himself in somewhat daring female poses with some hint or insinuation regarding his seriousness and purity."[4] "This book," explained

Don Giovanni, "must be published by a Milanese publisher"
with whom he had signed a contract, under which the priest
would receive the sum of five thousand lire upon consignment
of the manuscript, but would have to pay the same amount as
a penalty "if he decides not to live up to his commitment to finish and send the pamphlet." Repenting that he had signed the
agreement, the canon confided to the teacher that he wanted to
find a solution to get himself out of trouble without damaging
the stigmatized religious, but he added that he did not have
at hand the money to pay the penalty[5]. The woman believed
him and, "compelled by a feeling of devotion toward the pious
Capuchin, and her desire to spare him afflictions," hurried to
report the incident to Emanuele Brunatto[6], "whom she knew"
and whom she considered "had great affection for the person
of Padre Pio" and invited him to assume the task of dealing
with the priest. The two met and, "during an initial talk," after
having confirmed the "existence and the damaging content of
the booklet, the Canon Miscio repeated the offer of not giving
it to the press upon monetary compensation."[7] But Emmanuele
Brunatto explained to him: "The family of Padre Pio is absolutely
incapable of paying a similar amount, since it lives in complete
poverty."[8] The negotiations went on for some time until the priest
gave an *ultimatum*: "The money, if you want to protect Padre
Pio, must be consigned before and not after January 2! By way of
compensation, the claim has been modestly lessened, and from
the initial five thousand lire it went down to four thousand."

Understanding that the dialog had already come to the
end of the line, Brunatto felt it his duty to inform the family of
Padre Pio which, obviously, remained deeply disturbed. Michele
Forgione, the elder brother of the friar, after an initial moment
of disorientation, asked help from the informer to "anticipate

the money needed to silence the blackmailer." The designated person, however, did more than the mandate received and, knowing that generally "a blackmailer, once paid, must then be paid ever after," showed himself "disposed to pay Miscio the sum requested, or at least a good part of it"[9] but, at the same time, he decided to turn to the police, hoping "that the carabinieri would be interested in surprising and arresting the criminals": Canon Miscio and his brother Vincenzo. Brigadier Casavola did not show himself in accord with this plan of action. So Brunatto decided to act alone. On the morning of January 5, 1926, prior to the appointment, he met Don Giovanni and handed him the three thousand lire in cash. The priest took them and even signed "a receipt, in which he declared to have received from Michele Forgione the said sum, committing himself not to proceed with the publication harming the honor of a person in his family." "In the evening of the same day," the intermediary "presented himself to the Sub-Official, showing him a receipt of L. 3,000 signed by Canon Giovanni Miscio, denouncing him as the author of the said extortion in the absence of his brother Vincenzo."[10] Brigadier Casavola, "after hearing the other witnesses" and "gathering the necessary proofs to act," went to the house of the priest, found and sequestered the manuscript and arrested its author.[11]

Five days later the whole town was informed of the incident by *La Gazzetta di Puglia* and by *Il Giornale d'Italia*. This last daily also specified that Padre Pio "remained perfectly unaware of the affair, and when he came to know about it he felt a tremendous shock and he almost fainted."[12] He tried every way to convince Emmanuele Brunatto and her brother Michele to withdraw the lawsuit without succeeding in making them stop their resolve.

The process ended "on the evening of December 2" 1926, at a late hour. The Tribunal, having verified "that the mendacious affirmations that the publication had already been decided on and contracted for with an imaginary editorial house and that the withdrawal of the sum of 5,000 lire to pay the penalty was necessary," in truth were intended to give life to those scams designed to deceive other people's good faith and belief whereas the goal of the canon was "to gain from the scheme some profit, perhaps driven to it by the mania for riches and by the prodigality of the convent," declared "Giovanni Miscio guilty of fraud punishable with three months of imprisonment, a fine of 1,000 lire, for damages liquidated in lire, in conformity with civil demands, and for the expenses of the trial with suspension of the sentence or condemnation for five years, modifying the rubric of the offence into fraud. It absolved the other defendant Vincenzo Miscio, brother of the canon for lack of proofs. Against the sentence pronounced, the defense of the Miscio brothers made appeal. Even the P.M., Cavalier Cuccurullo, made appeal, believing that the matter was one of extortion, not of fraud."[13] The night preceding the start of the process at the second level, "the lawyer of the brother of Padre Pio against Miscio – the Hon. Caprile – came to S. Giovanni Rotondo, to Padre Pio, who entertained him in his cell for about an hour. Upon leaving, the lawyer knelt down in the middle of the door to kiss his hand, to be blessed and to bid him farewell. Padre Pio, being resolute, takes his hands and clasps them inside his own, and says: 'So, do you promise me you will not let Don Giovanni be condemned?' The lawyer answers: 'But, Padre, how can I go against my client (the brother of Padre Pio)? I would be failing in my duty.' To which Padre Pio replied: 'I have spoken and I command you not to let the priest be condemned.' And after so many backs and forths, yeses and noes, the lawyer answers: 'Padre Pio, since you want it, I will do all I can to mitigate those charges and save the priest.' So Padre Pio told him that he could leave, and accompanied him until the stairs. There he made him repeat his promise and then dismissed him."[14]

In spite of the commitment of the lawyer Caprile, "the Court of Appeals of Bari accepts the recourse of the Public Ministry and changes the sentence to twenty months of imprisonment. The Supreme Court of Cassation rejected a final appeal of the accused, while the Ministry of Pardon and Justice, due to the offensive nature of the crime, did not allow the petition for mercy presented by the same Canon Miscio to proceed."[15]

Following the sentence, the priest lost "his position as an elementary school teacher" and, once again, Padre Pio intervened in his favor, writing "a petiton to His Majesty, King Vittorio Emanuele III, asking that he might return to teaching, and he obtained it. Miscio was very grateful for this, thanking Padre Pio, and once in a while he came to visit him till he was late in age in spite of his ailments."[16]

Monsignor Pasquale Gagliardi

Monsignor Pasquale Gagliardi[17] has been defined as "the sworn enemy of Padre Pio who will 'preside' at the defamatory campaign against the Capuchin from the Twenties to the Thirties of the Nineteen Hundreds."[18] His prejudices gave rise to a correction on the part of Benedict XV.

Already under the pontificate of Pope Benedict XV, in fact, Padre Pio began to be an object of calumnies and attacks. The first was a report written on April 19, 1919 to Monsignor Carlo

Perosi, assessor of the Holy Office by Padre Agostino Gemelli upon returning from San Giovanni Rotondo where he had not been allowed to see the stigmata of the Capuchin. In the document, though admitting that "Padre Pio is truly a man of elevated exemplary religiosity," the friar-doctor, after having described the stigmata in the hands as if he had seen them, in spite of having specified in his Preface of not having performed "any examination from the medical point of view," testified: "To the undersigned it seems that it is a case of suggestion unconsciously produced by Padre Benedetto in a sick subject like Padre Pio and that has led to those characteristic manifestations of psittacism typical of the hysterical structure."[19] The second attack came from the deposition of two Foggia pharmacists, Doctor Valentini-Vista and his cousin Maria De Vito, from whom the Capuchin had asked for two caustic substances: carbolic acid and veratridine. Suspecting that he could use them to acquire the now well-known wounds, the two pharmacists manifested their doubts to the bishop of Foggia, Monsignor Salvatore Bella, who had them put their story in black and white and send it, on July 24, 1920, to the Holy Offfice.[20]

Soon after the arrival of the report of Padre Gemelli, on May 29, 1920, a man who was trusted by the Pope and the Cardinal Secretary of State, Pietro Gasparri, Monsignor Bonaventura Cerretti, Secretary for Extraordinary Affairs of the Secretariat of State and Consultor of the Supreme Congregation, was sent to San Giovanni Rotondo[21]. The prelate presented himself at the convent with a "letter of the Holy Office."[22] On July 12, 1920 another collaborator of the Secretary of State, the Passionist Padre Luigi Besi, who among other things had been the postulator of Gemma Galgani, arrived accompanied by the personal doctor of the Pope.[23] Evidently, both visits[24] received favorable reviews regarding the Capuchin since the Pope in person reprimanded the archbishop of Manfredonia, Monsignor Pasquale Gagliardi, who showed himself very skeptical towards Padre Pio, explaining to him: "It is good to proceed cautiously, but it is bad to show yourself to be so incredulous."[25]

The benevolence of Benedict XV did not prevent the Holy Office from working to get greater clarity regarding the case, sending to San Giovanni Rotondo an Apostolic Visitor, with the task of carrying out "an accurate investigation."[26] It was the Holy Father who chose the prelate to whom the delicate task was entrusted: the discalced Carmelite Monsignor Carlo Raffaello Rossi, at that time bishop of Volterra[27], who reached his destination prejudiced against the Capuchin.[28] At the end, however, he became edified. In fact, at the end of his investigation, he wrote to the Supreme Congregation that: "Padre Pio is a good religious; regarding the 'graces' sought, as it is said, through his prayers, many do not exist, others are only affirmed, but there are no juridical proofs; regarding the extraordinary taking place in the person of Padre Pio, one cannot say how it happens, but it certainly does not happen by diabolical intervention, deceit or fraud."[29]

In spite of all that, hardly three months after the election of the new Pope, Pius XI, on May 10, 1922, "the General Inquisitors of the Holy Office" decided "to write a letter to the Minister General of the Capuchins," giving orders that Padre Pio "not celebrate Mass at a fixed hour but at any hour, preferably very early in the morning and in private; […] that for no reason is he to show the so-called stigmata, or talk about them or allow people to kiss them"; that he be assigned a "spiritual director other than Padre Benedetto da San Marco in Lamis, with whom he will cease any communication, even through letters." In the document, moreover, the need was expressed that the stigmatized friar "be sent far from San Giovanni Rotondo and assigned to another place." Finally, all this should be done in such a way "that on the part of Padre Pio or of others for him, letters addressed to him by devout persons looking for advice or for other motives"[30] no longer be answered. It is too easy to hypothesize that in the judgment of the cardinals, the report of Gemelli, friend of the new Pope, carried more weight than the conclusions of the "vote" of Monsignor Rossi. In truth, the cardinals only shared and approved the proposals that the seven consultors had expressed in their "vote" on the first of May 1922.[31]

The consideration of Pius XI at the start of his pontificate, at any rate, was certainly not the same as that of his predecessor since, on "July 3, 1922, during a private audience [...] he ordered Monsignor Gagliardi, archbishop of Manfredonia, not to go to San Giovanni Rotondo 'out of prudence.'"[32]

To complicate things even further was a letter dated July 12, 1922 from the same Monsignor Gagliardi to the Supreme Congregation in which he asserted that "twice recently the Capuchin Fathers of the convent of San Giovanni Rotondo fought and struck each other to the point of drawing blood with steel weapons and firearms, and some of them were wounded," all over the "distribution of the large sums accumulated by Padre Pio."[33] To this, the Archbishop of Manfredonia also added accusations of immorality regarding the friars. The Holy See asked for clarifications from the Minister General of the Capuchins who, the same month, sent Padre Celestino da Desio to the place, "for an accurate canonical visit," from which it emerged that the "Fathers are purely victims of the envy of some bad-intentioned people, who see with evil eyes the great amount of good done by those religious, and to paralyze it they enjoy inventing things that are totally false." And, to ascertain the truth, it was enough for him to have a brief talk with the "Marshal of the Carabinieri" who testified: "I have never been called to the convent, neither to be certain, nor to settle the quarrel in question. I have indeed heard the news that circulated in the town, but I have not given it any importance. I shall say more: knowing well the Fathers of the convent, I said to myself quickly: This is a pure invention."[34] At this point a new request for clarification was sent to Monsignor Gagliardi, explaining that it had received accusations regarding the friars from Canon Domenico Palladino, from whom there was a hurry to ask for a "clarification of the facts." From the report of the informing priest, attached to the letter of the diocesan pastor, it was discovered that he had never been a direct witness of the "battle in the convent," but had heard of it talked about by "some farmers" who mentioned to him "all the din, the shouts that the friars and others were making in the garden, the flash of some firearms, the appearance of Padre Pio to calm the quarrel, the trip of the Marshal to the place of the convent, etc."[35] For all practical purposes, a rumor had become the motive for a denunciation to the Holy Office signed by the archbishop.

New letters with other charges continued to be sent to the Vatican from Manfredonia. Thus the need for a new examination of the situation entrusted, on the basis of the documents, to the Carmelite Padre Lorenzo di San Basilio, consultor of the Supreme Congregation. His report, printed in March 1923, evidenced "the difficult atmosphere that had set in between the friars of the convent of San Giovanni Rotondo and the local parish priests, among whom the most relentless was Canon Palladino supported, in this sense, by Bishop Gagliardi."[36] He then pointed out the failure to follow, even if out of "good faith on the part of the Padre Provincial," the prohibition of the Holy Office for Padre Pio to respond to letters and above all the complete non-compliance of the directive to transfer him to another convent, insinuating the doubt that the person concerned had not clearly expressed his availability to follow the order.[37] In reality, there was created a popular movement ready "to have recourse to any means, even an extreme one, if any attempt to move the stigmatized Capuchin is made."[38]

In the eyes of the consultor, therefore, "the situation in San Giovanni Rotondo had become so critical as to require urgent and energetic measures."[39]

And the most energetic measures were not long in coming: on May 31, 1923 "the Supreme Congregation of the Holy Office charged with the protection of faith and morals, upon carrying out an investigation of the events attributed to Padre Pio da Pietrelcina [...] declares that from the aforesaid investigation the supernaturality of the same events do not result and exhorts the faithful to conform to this declaration in their behavior."[40] Also some orders were transmitted to the Capuchins, among which the obligation to let the friar of Pietrelcina celebrate "in the inner chapel of the convent, not allowing persons to assist there" and the prohibition to answer "whether through him or through others" those letters that are addressed to him from devoted persons for the purpose of advice, out of gratitude, or for other motives."[41] On June 25 Padre Pio said Mass for the first time in private. But it remained the only time, because "a crowd of about 3,000 persons, preceded by a band, the authorities of the town and by various associations with their standards" went on the same day "to the convent to protest and to make threats in order to obtain an immediate revocation of the order."[42] The Guardian of the Friary was forced to suspend the implementation of the measure.

In July 30 the transfer of Padre Pio to Ancona was decided upon. But here again nothing was done on account of the

"Fascist threats": "We shall crucify Padre Pio and the Father Guardian of the friary!"[43]

Prompted by the Supreme Congregation to resolve the problem, the Minister General of the Order turned to General De Bono, the Director General of Public Security, who sent to the place the functionary Carmelo Camilleri. Camilleri understood immediately the situation and reported that, to send the Capuchin away from San Giovanni Rotondo, "an action of force would be needed and there will be shedding of blood for sure."

On May 15, 1924 the commissioner of the religious Province of Sant'Angelo-Foggia of the Friars Minor Capuchins, Padre Bernardo d'Alpicella, went to the Episcopate in Manfredonia. To him Bishop Gagliardi said: "I swear on my priesthood to have seen with my eyes Padre Pio powdering his face in his room, when I was at San Giovanni Rotondo for a holy visit. The Padre felt uncomfortable being caught red-handed, so much so that he felt ashamed to present himself during recreation time after lunch."[44] Speaking of which, Padre Ignazio da Ielsi, in his diary, recalled that "To have surprised Padre Pio is a true calumny. The monsignor reached the convent after 8'oclock in the morning, when Padre Pio was already in the confessional. He saw Padre Pio a little before 10 o'clock, that is, when the Padre, dispatched from the confessions, went to see him in the room where the monsignor was conversing with the Very Rev. Padre Agostino da San Marco. There Padre Pio kissed the hand of the monsignor and the monsignor, lifting the glove, kissed the wound in the hand of Padre Pio. The latter left immediately to say Mass and he was not seen anymore by the monsignor except toward 3 p.m., when he went into town."[45]

On July 24, 1924 the Holy Office expressed itself in an unambiguous manner: "Having now gathered, from even more numerous and reliable sources, other information, the same Supreme Sacred Congregation retains it its sacred duty to exhort the faithful with even more serious words, so that they may absolutely abstain from visiting him and having any rapport with him, even by letter, for reasons of devotion."[46]

The following year the religious Province was placed under commission. In San Giovanni Rotondo, meanwhile, the thought came of fighting the enemies of the friar with their same weapons and there was a move "to gather documents and testimonies to prove the truth of the phenomena related to Padre Pio and even to reveal the corruption of the personalities who denigrated and accused Padre Pio." At the end of June 1925 Emanuele Brunatto left for Rome with "two voluminous dossiers" and met with Don Luigi Orione, who advised him "to make copies of them to be handed over to each Cardinal member of the Holy Office."[47] This he did. The initiative, however, did not have any effect. At this point Brunatto, using the pseudonym of Giuseppe De Rossi, translated those documents into a book which he published in 1926 and which was put on the *Index* at once.

This time there was an effect. In 1927 the Holy See sent an apostolic visitor with the task of looking into what was happening in the Archdiocese. The visitor, Bishop Felice Bevilacqua, chose as collaborator precisely Brunatto. Bevilacqua, however, did not finish his task, because he was called back to Rome to work on a new inquiry "within the environs of the Papal Household."[48] Even in this case he made use of the help of Brunatto. In Manfredonia, however, Bishop Giuseppe Bruno finished the work. His conclusions, accepted "by the very eminent cardinals of the Congregation on May 23, 1929"[49] prompted Cardinal Carlo Perosi to invite Bishop Gagliardi to resign. His letter of resignation was signed on October 1.[50] By now approaching his seventieth year, the archbishop returned to his town of origin, in Tricarico, in the province of Matera, from where "he often wrote to the convent of the Capuchins in San Giovanni Rotondo, asking for holy Mass intentions with a relative offering. They were always allowed" and "the one who most favored that work of charity was precisely he": Padre Pio. Moreover, when Padre Raffaele da Sant'Elia a Pianisi informed him of the death of Bishop Gagliardi which took place on November 11, 1941, the stigmatized Capuchin said: "Tomorrow I shall celebrate Mass in his suffrage."[51]

Monsignor Carlo Maccari

At the end of the 1950s in San Giovanni Rotondo a confrontation between a group of laypeople connected with the Casa Sollievo della Sofferenza and some friars was created. The bone of contention between the two factions had to do with affection for Padre Pio and the destination of the "free offerings", that is, of those sent to Padre Pio without specification as to their destination.

The issue ended up getting the attention of the Holy Office. Cardinal Ottaviani, Secretary of the Supreme Congregation, "commanded the Reverend Padre Bonaventura da Pavullo, the Definitor General of the Capuchins in the Italian peninsula, to go to San Giovanni Rotondo to make an inquiry and then to report."[52] From his visit came a report in which Padre Pio was described as "righteous, simple, delicate," hard working at an "onerous and precious spiritual work," but it also placed in evidence "an implacable and undue interference on the part of civilians in the affairs of the convent, in what concerns even the private life of Padre Pio" who, for his part, was "inclined to think well and did not consider himself as going overboard in supporting and defending, when necessary, those who for him are only his affectionate children and faithful collaborators." To strengthen this thesis another report was sent spontaneously to the Holy See by Angelo Battisti who, besides being the Administrator of the Casa Sollievo della Sofferenza, was also an employee of the Secretariat of State and that of the Archbishop of Manfredonia, Monsignor Andrea Cesarano, who asked a series of questions: "Who and what persons receive this money? And for what purpose is it given? Where does it end up? How has it been spent? How is it used?"[53] There were, therefore, sufficient grounds to demand greater clarity.

But the Holy Office, during the pontificate of John XXIII, continued to follow the line of discretion. During the Plenary of March 12, 1960 it was decided to send to the town of Gargano Monsignor Mario Crovini, Substitute in the Section of Book Censorship at the Dicastery and a friend of Battisti, for a 'secret' visit […] camouflaged under the pretext of a clinical analysis,"[54] in order to "talk with Padre Pio and to hear from him about the problems and how to solve them […] without making interrogations, probes or inquisitions."[55]

But before Monsignor Crovini could start his mission, on April 14 the Minister General of the Capuchins, Padre Clemente da Milwaukee had written a letter to the Pope asking him "to send to San Giovanni Rotondo, as soon as possible, an Apostolic Visitation" in order to "prevent some big scandal of a religious and financial nature that might take place" because of "a dangerous situation that was emerging in San Giovanni Rotondo around the venerable person of Padre Pio and, unfortunately, often in his name."[56]

Padre Clemente further specified in an attachment that "the most serious drawbacks are taking place, especially concerning the hospital work in the 'Casa Sollievo della Sofferenza'"[57]: "The Council of Administration has almost never met and everything is decided arbitrarily by some elements who take advantage of the trust of Padre Pio, who physically finds it impossible to handle this financial and technical part of his Work. These lay people receive, open, and answer the correspondence, even personal, of Padre Pio, which often contains delicate cases of conscience; they withdraw the offerings, but it is not known to whom they render due detailed account […]. The intrusion, the arbitrariness and the independence of the lay people – even in spiritual matters such as for example the prayer groups – have come to the point of pressuring civil and church authorities, local and Roman, against anyone who attempts to regulate their way of acting, to silence them or keep them away from San Giovanni Rotondo. They try their best – so they say – to allow Padre Pio to leave the convent and to retire in the 'Casa Sollievo della Sofferenza'."[58] The document ended with these very serious words: "Those lay people have created an environment of pseudo-mysticism and sometimes of evident fanaticism very often combined with real profiteering even if it is skillfully screened."[59]

John XXIII, on April 30, gave an audience to the Minister General, who went to the pontiff accompanied by Padre Bonaventura. The Holy Father "received them in his private study with fatherly kindness and familiarity" and, after having listened to them, revealed that he "had a great esteem for Padre Pio, even though he had never seen him, and that he was not surprised that there were some troublesome persons and profiteers around him and his work. That always happens: where something good is being done, the enemy can be expected to be there too; he is not idle. His Holiness promised to send a visitor and the Father General had the tactfulness to add: 'Holy Father, we would desire that the visitor not belong to our Order, to keep away every suspicion of partiality.' The Pope smiled and said: "Very well. It is only right that it be so."[60]

Also arriving at the same conclusion, on June 1, were the Cardinals of the Supreme Congregation after having examined the report written by Monsignor Crovini at the end of his mission which was carried out between 18 and 28 of April, and they decided to place the issue "in the hands of the Secretariat of State which will provide an Apostolic Delegate (or Visitor), with the task of watching over the general progress and especially to receive, sort out, and control the correspondence and the offerings."[61] During the following meeting on June 8 they named as "Apostolic Visitor Monsignor Bontempi, then Rector of the Nepomuceno College. But on the 28th Monsignor Bontempi withdrew from the task."[62]

In the meantime the magnetic reels of some local "tapings" had reached the Holy Office made by two friars of the convent of San Giovanni Rotondo[63] and by Monsignor Umberto Terenzi, rector and parish priest of the Roman sanctuary Divino Amore, a devout visitor to the convent of San Giovanni Rotondo,[64] in which the authors of the tapings recognized having heard the smack of a kiss during a conversation between Padre Pio and a spiritual daughter of his.[65]

At this point the Supreme Congregation bypassed every delay and, upon the proposal of the Secretary of State, Cardinal Domenico Tardini,[66] on July 13, 1960 "Mons. Carlo Maccari, Secretary of the Vicariate,[67] was nominated Apostolic Visitor"; John XXIII, on the evening of July 19, wanted to meet the delegate in the Vatican gardens to tell him: "The 'plenary' session of the Holy Office has unanimously chosen you for an arduous and delicate task: a choice approved and blessed by me, because I nourish

a lively trust that you will commit yourself to the serious task
entrusted to you with responsibility, spirit of faith and service to
the truth. It is an ecclesial task, which you have not looked for:
hence, accept it with great serenity and abandonment to the grace
of the Lord!" He exhorted the Visitor to "not separate himself
from the golden rule: *to see everything, to correct in charity.*"[68]

Then he continued "focusing on the object of the visit
with precise references to persons, situations and tensions,"[69]
explaining that the objective of the mission was to "liberate –
with the consent of the legitimate Superiors – the priestly action
of Padre Pio from pressures, passions, abuses, and so make it
more peaceful and fruitful."[70] He did not fail to express his
thoughts regarding the Capuchin: "What to think […] about
this religious, who certainly does good but not succeeding in
dissipating shadows and doubts around his alleged holiness?
In recent times the shadows have increased and the doubts
have become more serious."[71] The Pope, finally, asked "to be
informed in detail" about the visit and "its difficulties," recommending to Monsignor Maccari to "proceed gradually and
with patience, frankness and cordiality, towards everybody but
especially towards Padre Pio."[72]

Only after some months would the Holy Father have been
made aware of the "absolute and personal," "singular and over-
bearing" character of him who had been chosen for this delicate
mission,[73] even if some "complaints regarding his hardness and
fussiness in dealing with the priests in the Vicariate" had reached
him "even before this nomination."[74] But these voices did not
prevail in comparison with the authoritative opinion of the closest
collaborators of the Pope. Monsignor Loris Francesco Capovilla,
his personal secretary, knew Maccari "when he was secretary of
the Vicariate of the City, an active coordinator of the activities of

the First Roman Synod called by John XXIII" and soon nourished "towards him sentiments of esteem for his priestly piety, his culture, his stately bearing, and his industriousness. Before entering the Offices of the Vicariate he had been an excellent suburban pastor and animator of Catholic Action and charitable work. In the sixties he enjoyed the trust of the senior employees of the Pope, who looked to him as a 'man of God accomplished and thoroughly equipped for every good work': strict with himself and with others, inflexible guardian of orthodoxy, convinced upholder of Church discipline."[75] The mission of Monsignor Maccari certainly did not start out on the right foot. The Provincial Minister holding office at that time, Padre Amedeo Fabrocini, testified:

"On the night of July 29, 1960 Padre Bonaventura da Pavullo, the Definitor General, called me up in Foggia, telling me to take the midnight train and to go to Caserta, where I found him waiting for me. In a very short conversation, less than a quarter of an hour, at the train station in Caserta, Padre Bonaventura said to me: 'An Apostolic Visitor will be arriving in Foggia in the early hours of the morning. Receive him with much deference. Collaborate with all that he asks of you. Create some spectacle and organize some event honoring him. Ocassionally invite him to lunch.' Still in Caserta, in the short talk he had with me, Padre Bonaventura da Pavullo said to me that if the Apostolic Visitor had hinted at the tape recorders installed in #5, the small room of Padre Pio and in the guests' quarters on the groundfloor, where Padre Pio and the other religious gathered to talk with the faithful, of the two installed, one should be taken away, allowing the other to work (I don't remember well if Padre Bonaventura told me to unplug the one installed in cell #5 or the one in the guests' quarters on the groundfloor). After our brief conversation, I quickly took the train for Foggia, which however reached its destination after that of Monsignor Carlo Maccari. So I was not present at the arrival of the said Monsignor in Foggia (convent of the Immaculate) to receive him and to pay my respects.

Besides, it must be borne in mind that the official communication of the Padre General sent to me was dated August 1, 1960, that is, some days after the arrival of Monsignor Carlo Maccari.

Towards nine in the morning of July 30, Monsignor Carlo Maccari, who did not wait for my arrival, reached Manfredonia, on a visit to Archbishop Andrea Cesarano. After some hours, he called me up from the diocesan curia, announcing that he had already arrived, and with an irritated voice he reproached me for not being anywhere in the convent of the Immaculata.

I answered that I had not been informed on time about his arrival and that I was out of my residence.

Mons. Maccari replied: 'But how can that be? Didn't Padre Bonaventura mail you a letter?' And I: 'I have not received anything' (in fact, I had not received any letter).

Monsignor Carlo Maccari: 'At any rate, today (July 30, 1960) at 3 p.m. be there at the convent of San Giovanni Rotondo.'

Punctual for the appointment, I instructed a religious to watch at the door of the convent with the task of informing me on time as soon as he saw a priest in the square, because I wanted to be sure to receive him at the entrance of the convent. Instead, the religious, being distracted by something unexpected, did not notice the arrival of the Apostolic Visitor and did not see him in the square in front of the convent."[76]

Monsignor Maccari did not take it well at all. "When, around 6 in the afternoon, the Visitor came down in front of the new temple of Holy Mary of the Graces," he testified in his report, "he was received by Commander Angelo Battisti who in the morning had already come to Manfredonia to pay his respects: neither the Provincial – who also had been advised by telephone – nor the Superior of the convent, nor any other Padre was present. Made to enter the enclosure by the religious serving at the door, I had to wait for about ten minutes inside a small room, before the Provincial arrived."[77]

The rest of the story is also taken from the recollections of Padre Amedeo:

> "As soon as I was notified, I was urged to go to pay my respects to the Apostolic Visitor, excusing myself for the inconvenience.
> I found him frowning. I asked if he had some dispositions to give.
> And the Monsignor said: 'Gather the community together.'
> And I: 'Including Padre Pio?'
> Monsignor: 'Including Padre Pio.'
> Once the community was gathered in the refectory, Monsignor asked me if I had wanted to say something.
> I declined the invitation, not knowing the specific motive of the presence of the Monsignor.
> So he began speaking and, with an almost fatherly tone, said that he had come as Apostolic Visitor. Then he exhorted everybody to be at peace, affirming that they would have found him very understanding.
> Upon knowing the purpose of his presence, I also began to speak and promised docility and full collaboration, in homage to the Supreme Authority and to the person of the Visitor.
> When the brief session was dissolved, Monsignor Maccari, privately and with an irritated voice reprimanded me because I had given the task of waiting for him at the door of the convent to a religious, instead of waiting for him personally.
> And he added, referring to what had happened a short while ago in the refectory: 'And be aware that the last one to talk is me and not you.'"[78]

The Apostolic Visit took place from July 30 to the end of September[79] with two interruptions.

Monsignor Maccari had the impression that the Capuchin with the stigmata held toward him, "an attitude that was not only closed, suspicious and cold, but [...] almost hostile," that the delegate of the Holy Office believed that must be attributed to the "state of mind of the religious suffering and subjected to other Visits of the kind, mainly 'fomented' by nearby and far-away persons who – in good faith or for a complex of reasons, not all noble and disinterested – seemed to do everything to make my task 'hateful.'"[80] Twelve years later, however, the same Visitor admitted "that the attitude of the Padre could have contributed to a certain manner of proceeding, on my part, perhaps too intent on discovering the truth with steps and a style that seem to me to be always generously chosen but perhaps sometimes too 'sincere' and maybe irritating."[81] Therefore, not according to the directives received from John XXIII.

All together, Monsignor Maccari questioned Padre Pio eight times. The investigated, more than about himself, thought about his spiritual daughters, deprived suddenly of his fatherly guidance: "But why must those poor creatures be prohibited from having what is granted to others? If the Lord has entrusted them to me (expression many times repeated), I cannot leave them in that way... After all, what harm have they done? [...] I saw them being born, you can say, as good daughters whom the Lord has entrusted to me; they are souls who have cost the blood of the Heart of Jesus..."[82] But the prelate coming from Rome judged this answer as an expression of a "wall of resistance," and, making recourse to the authority of the one who had sent him to San Giovanni Rotondo, answered: "Are you not aware that, continuing to give credit and trust to those who declare themselves as enemies of the Pope's representative, you yourself are considered as an accomplice and in a certain sense an inspirer of this fight? I must, therefore, conclude that you are rebelling against the Holy See?" "But for the love of God, Monsignor!" was the answer. "Were they even my father and my mother, should they do this, they would be acting badly… and I would condemn them…"[83]

The investigator's approach toward the elderly Capuchin was anything but serene and this was only one of the critical points of his visit. Although taking into account that from the environment of San Giovanni Rotondo sprang up "flights of fantasy, rumors collected and exaggerated, endless chatter and gossip,"[84] Monsignor Maccari gathered any number of statements that he could not verify nor did he believe it opportune to do so. Moreover, he did not think it opportune to question the official Provincial Minister[85] or the Guardian who, in the previous six years, had been the immediate superior of the "person being investigated."[86]

Both certainly could have been able to say a few words in defense of Padre Pio. He did not even let Dr. Francesco Lotti testify, although he had been presented to him as the "dean of the doctors of the Casa Sollievo,"[87] just as he did not call Dr. Giuseppe Sala, the attending physician taking care of the Capuchin.[88] They were also admirers of Padre Pio. In other words, "the witnesses who could have known the truth were not called: some were deliberately excluded."[89] Instead, "on one of the first days of the visit, Maccari invited to dinner" a priest, "one of the survivors of the early days who belonged to the group that plotted all sorts of slanders against Padre Pio… Thus it was easy for him to dig up all the rotten matters of the past. Proof of this is that the next morning all of the most suspect and notorious individuals who were part of the group of priests of the early days [who had sided] against Padre Pio began to go to see the visitor."[90] Against this background, the outcome of the visit was to be expected.

The Monsignor, having finished his task, left for Rome where, apparently, he reported to the Pope the news that certainly were not positive about the Capuchin of San Giovanni Rotondo. John XXIII, in fact, on September 9, in his agenda, after having noted his meeting with the Visitor, commented: "Unfortunately, p. p. [Padre Pio] is shown to be an *idol of straw. Spare us, O Lord. Spare your people.*"[91]

It has not been possible to reconstruct the information behind such a serious judgment, but it is easy to hypothesize that Monsignor Maccari had sent to the Pope an advance copy of the contents of his report:

"There is today a veritable industry that lives and prospers on the propaganda regarding the 'holiness' of the 'first stigmatized priest'."[92]

"A very skillful and unscrupulous propaganda, which, basing itself on religious ignorance rampant in every social order, would have known how to exploit the easy enthusiasm and ingenuous gullibility for anything that smacks of the 'miraculous,' and then gradually would have created the myth of the 'holy miracle worker,' who is untouchable, called by God for an 'extraordinary and mysterious mission,' in the whole Church; thus one arrives at 'venerating' the 'first stigmatized priest' in history, as the most perfect 'reincarnation of Christ' and to admire him as 'the most loving, purest and most humble of all human beings.'"[93]

"Once these convictions are admitted [...] it is inevitable that religious concepts oscillating between superstition and magic, the idolatrous cult of the person, and certain behaviors that can lead to heretical deviations may arise and become widespread, under the name of the celebrated Capuchin."[94]

"All this atmosphere of the falsely supernatural... is none other than the fruit of a colossal and widespread organization in the hands of a very few spiritual daughters who, in their turn are aided by and supported blindly by other men and women [...] It is true to say that the interested party is often completely in the dark about a machine that is becoming ever more mastodontic bringing to the whole world his reputation for 'sanctity' and 'miracles.'"[95]

Unable to deny that "the mercy of the Lord has triumphed for so many years and still prevails in many souls through the ministry of this Capuchin [...] and the benefits derived from it [...] present themselves with the characteristics of something not common due to their extension in time and space," the Visitor asked himself: "If this man is not living internally the life of sanctity that the multitude of his 'devotees' attribute to him, why has the loving providence of God permitted so much deception and has granted to such an imperfect instrument the ability to accomplish such a vast and enduring good work?"[96] But he managed to find an explanation even for this. The reason why Padre Pio, "having lived almost always in the convent with a rather modest culture, managed to lead a virtually 'second life,' without ever betraying himself, thus deceiving innumerable ranks of believers, some of whom are intelligent and cultured," can be identified with "what could be called the 'dual personality' of religious."[97]

While the visit was taking place, Giovanni Gigliozzi, a journalist from Radio Rai and a spiritual son of Padre Pio, seeing the friar cry because of the effects of the decisions and conduct of the delegate of the Holy See, said to the Capuchin being investigated: "Padre, you know that I know Monsignor Maccari. And I would like to say something that might be useful for you." Padre Pio answered: "It is useless, my son. Monsignor is now sick with cardinalitis. He will never be a Cardinal; but in heaven I want him to be beside me."[98]

On October 22, 1996 Monsignor Maccari, Archbishop of Ancona-Osimo, was seriously wounded in a road accident near Campocavallo di Osimo, while returning to Ancona by car. He stayed for six months in the hospital before dying on April 17, 1997. "During his long and painful illness" the former Apostolic Visitor "usually following the Litany of Loreto, would invoke the help of the friar with the stigmata and fatherly reprimanded the sisters who recited the prayers with him when they had forgotten his requests for help from Padre Pio."[99]

This news was also confirmed "by the Capuchin Padre Silvio Angeletti. As chaplain of the regional Hospital of Ancona, he testified that during his illness Monsignor Maccari asked for prayers and constantly invoked Padre Pio. In the last days of his life, he insistently and loudly invoked him even in a loud voice."[100] Corroborating this version, finally, are the words of Monsignor Nicola Larivera, who had been Vicar General of the diocese of Ancona for 14 years guided by Monsignor Maccari: "I can testify that Monsignor Maccari recently made an open profession of his profound veneration for Padre Pio."[101]

Monsignor Maccari never became a Cardinal, but his change of heart toward Padre Pio must have enabled him to be welcomed by the holy Capuchin on the threshold of paradise.

A Spiritual Daughter

Among the "gossip"[102] collected by Monsignor Carlo Maccari during his Apostolic Visit, there was the testimony of a woman of

San Giovanni Rotondo who, conventionally, we shall call Martha, about whom the same Apostolic Visitor noticed and noted "feelings of 'envy' and 'revenge'" and "the hint of an understandable female jealousy."[103] Nevertheless, in his report, the Visitor wrote:

> "According to [Martha], from 1922 to 1930 or so, Padre Pio da Pietrelcina would have had complete and prolonged 'intimate relations' with her, even several times a week; all this, however, would have happened without 'any malice' on one side or the other."[104]

This accusation has made credible in the eyes of Monsignor Maccari, also another:

> "Listening to [Martha], the 'intimate relations' with Padre Pio would be continued after 1930, with Cleonice Morcaldi, the third 'favorite.'"[105]

The apparent contradiction between "complete and prolonged relations" and the absence of "malice on one side or the other" should have been a clear indication of the psychological equilibrium of the accuser who, evidently, was obsessed by her "female jealousy" and was firmly determined to create a scandal. Martha, in fact, back in 1940 had convinced a friar to believe that Padre Pio had had a nocturnal encounter in church with Cleonice Morcaldi. This friar, in turn, caused the same suspicion to arise in another confrere as well.

These two Capuchins made their deposition to Monsignor Maccari, aggravating the position of Padre Pio.[106] The same Martha, moreover, revealed to the Visitor "of having mentioned in confession to Padre Raffaele her 'relations' with Padre Pio, making him also aware of reports that the same pious Padre had with

Cleonice, and authorizing him to make use of it, if he believed it to be opportune, even 'in the external forum'."[107] Finally, she also reported the same acts to Padre Umberto Terenzi, who repeated the story himself a second time, in order to make a record of it and then consign everything to the Holy Office.[108]

What should have been apparent to Monsignor Maccari was providentially explained by the Archbishop of Manfredonia, at the time, Monsignor Andrea Cesarano, in an interview with the Secretary of the Congregation, Cardinal Alfredo Ottaviani. "When His Eminence told him the name of the woman who had accused herself of having had carnal relations with Padre Pio," the Archbishop said: "She is a fanatic, a hysterical person! She does not merit being believed."[109] Only in this way were drastic measures against Padre Pio avoided.[110]

The vilified friar was informed of having been accused by Martha. Nina Campanile, the one who had been defined as "his first favorite"[111] revealed it to him in confession after having been questioned on the matter by Monsignor Maccari. The penitent was "surprised when the priest [Padre Pio] tried to excuse [Martha]" and she allowed "a resentful expression against the venerable Padre" to escape. He calmed her down, explaining to her: "My daughter, if we are not gentle, these souls will go straight to perdition." These words made Campanile understand "the enigma of the goal of the venerated Padre: to save souls, to save souls, even at the cost of being vilified."[112]

But the forgiveness of Padre Pio was absolute and went beyond his "teaching method" with the aim of helping his spiritual daughter to grow in faith. This was also corroborated by Nina Campanile while telling what happened at the start of February 1965, when Martha became ill and was hospitalized in the "Casa Sollievo della Sofferenza":

"She had received all the sacraments, but had wanted to confess another time, despite the fact that she had received Holy Communion early in the morning from Padre Innocenzo. After a little while she entered into a coma. None of her sisters was by her sick bed. Since a lot of snow had fallen, she had told them not to come. She died. But the priest stayed with her till the last. Some days after her death I asked Padre Pio: "Padre, was [Martha] saved?" He answered me: "Well, what do you think!? An act of perfect love cancels all sins."[113]

Moreover, when the relatives of the woman asked Padre Pio to write a thought on the holy remembrance card on the occasion of the thirtieth day following her death, with his stigmatized hand he wrote on the card:

"Her life was a continuous aspiration towards heaven and death found her prepared to meet Jesus. Now from on high she watches over those she has left in tears on earth."

And he signed the card: "Padre Pio, Capuchin."[114]

Notes for Chapter III

1. Mt 5:38-47.
2. "Regola bollata," chapter I, *Fonti francescane*, 75.
3. Cf. *Beatificationis et Canonizationis Servi Dei Pii a Pietrelcina. Positio super virtutibus*, Tipolitografia Signum, Bollate (MI) 1997, vol. III/1, p. 291.
4. "Motives of appeal presented by the Subsitute Procurator of the King, Cavalier Baldassarre Cuccurullo," in F. Chiocci, L. Cirri, *Padre Pio. Storia di una vittima*, I libri del NO, Rome 1967, vol. III, p. 167.
5. Cf. F. Chiocci, L. Cirri, *Padre Pio. Storia di una vittima*, op. cit., vol. I, pp. 439 and f.

6. Born in Turin on September 9, 1882 and died in Rome on February 10, 1965. He converted after he visited Padre Pio in 1920 and lived in the Capuchin convent until 1925; then he transferred to Pietrelcina. With his publications and his behavior he created not minor difficulties to the stigmatized Capuchin, to his confreres and to the Church.

7. Cf. *Positio super virtutibus*, op. cit., vol. III/1, p. 291.

8. F. Chiocci, L. Cirri, *Padre Pio. Storia di una vittima*, op. cit., vol. I, p. 440.

9. Cf. ibid, p. 441.

10. Cf. F. Chiocci, L. Cirri, *Padre Pio. Storia di una vittima*, op. cit., vol. III, pp. 164 and ff.

11. Cf. *Positio super virtutibus*, op. cit., vol. III/1, p. 291.

12. Anonymous, "Un canonico arrestato per tentata estorsione ad un frate ritenuto santo," in *Il Giornale d'Italia*, 10 January 1925, p. 6.

13. *Positio super virtutibus*, op. cit., vol. III/1, pp. 290-291.

14. "Testimony of Padre Raffaele da S. Elia a Pianisi," in *Positio super virtutibus*, op. cit., vol. II, p. 1522.

15. F. Chiocci, L. Cirri, *Padre Pio. Storia di una vittima*, op. cit., vol. I, p. 443.

16. "Testimony of Padre Raffaele da S. Elia a Pianisi," in *Positio super virtutibus*, op. cit., vol. II, p. 15.

17. Monsignor Pasquale Gagliardi was born in Tricarico, in the province of Matera, on December 7, 1859, of Rocco and Isabella Mattiace. At age 14 he received the ecclesiastical habit and entered the seminary for literary studies. He was ordained a priest in 1883. He was Archbishop of Manfredonia from November 7, 1897 to October 1, 1929. He died in his native city on December 11, 1941.

18. Cf. F. Castelli, *Padre Pio sotto inchiesta. "L'autobiografia segreta,"* Edizioni Ares, Milano 2008, p. 91.

19. G. Di Flumeri, *Il Beato Padre Pio da Pietrelcina*, Edizioni Padre Pio da Pietrelcina, San Giovanni Rotondo (FG) 2001, pp. 422 and ff.

20. Cf. S. Gaeta, A. Tornielli, *Padre Pio L'ultimo sospetto*, Piemme, Casale Monferrato (AL) 2008, pp. 51 and ff.; Cf. also "Vote of P. Lemius, Qualificator of the Holy Office," redacted on January 22, 1921 and printed in March of the same year, attachments II and III, in *Archivio della Congregazione per la Dottrina della Fede*.

21. Cf. *Annuario Pontificio*, Tipografia Poliglotta Vaticana, Roma 1918, p. 358.

22. Cf. *Positio super virtutibus*, vol. I/1, p. 408, n. 32.

23. Cf. ibid, 2.4.

24. It is not easy to establish if these had been true apostolic visits or non-official tasks. Castelli observes that "of them there is not any trace in the documentation kept in the Archives of the Congregation for the Doctrine of the Faith" (Cf. F. Castelli, *Padre Pio sotto inchiesta. "L'autobiografia segreta,"* op. cit., 93, note 21). But it cannot be excluded – in fact, seeing the role of the personalities involved, it is highly probable – that it had been the Pope in person that at that time was also the first in charge in the Holy Office, who sent Monsignor Cerretti and Padre Besi to San Giovanni Rotondo. It is therefore possible that both may have verbally referred their impression to the Holy Father or could have handed over their reports directly into his hands. This would explain the lack of corroborations in the archives of the Congregation.

25. Cf. *Positio super virtutibus*, op. cit., vol. I/1, p. 409.

26. "Vote of P. Lemius," op. cit., pp. 14 and ff.

27. Cf. M. Crovini, "Relazione (pro secreta) del marzo 1976," ds, S.O. 255/19, doc. 1225, p. 2, in *Archivio della Congregazione per la Dottrina della Fede.*

28. Cf. F. Castelli, *Padre Pio sotto inchiesta." L'autobiografia segreta,"* op. cit., p. 148.

29. Ibid, p. 155.

30. G. Di Flumeri, *Il Beato Padre Pio da Pietrelcina*, op. cit., p. 33.

31. Cf. "Report of P. Lorenzo di S. Basilio, Carmel. Discalced, Consultor," redacted on February 23, 1923 and printed in March of the same year, p. 3, in the *Archivio della Congregazione per la Dottrina della Fede.*

32. *Positio super virtutibus*, op. cit., vol. I/1, 111, n. 46.

33. "Report of P. Lorenzo di S. Basilio," op. cit., p. 26.

34. Ibid, pp. 29-30.

35. Ibid, p. 38.

36. "Report of Padre Cristoforo Bove, OFM Conv, Relatore," ds, December 19, 1996, p. 5, in *Archivio della Postulazione della Causa di Beatificazione e Canonizzazione di Padre Pio da Pietrelcina*, OFM Cap.; Cf. also "Report of P. Lorenzo di S. Basilio, op. cit., pp. 4 and ff.

37. Cf. "Report of Fr. Lorenzo di S. Basilio," pp. 9 and ff.

38. G. Saldutto, *Un tormentato settennio nella vita di Padre Pio da Pietrelcina*, Pontificia Universitas Gregoriana, Rome 1974, p. 151.

39. "Report of P. Lorenzo di S. Basilio," p. 4.

40. F. Spaccucci, *I cinque Papi di Padre Pio*, Laurenziana, Napoli 1968, p. 50. The Decree of the Holy Office was published by *L'Osservatore Romano* on July 5, 1923 and then taken up by a good part of the lay press.

41. "Letter of Padre Melchiorre da Benisa to Padre Pietro da Ischitella," Rome, June 11, 1923, in G. Saldutto, *Un tormentato settennio nella vita di Padre Pio da Pietrelcina*, op. cit., p. 165.

42. Ibid, p. 167.

43. G. Di Flumeri, *Il Beato Padre Pio*, op. cit., p. 36.

44. "Testimony of Padre Agostino da San Marco in Lamis," in *Positio super virtutibus*, op. cit., vol. III/1, p. 362; Cf. also I. da Ielsi, *Diario*, Marianna Iafelice (Ed.), Edizioni Padre Pio da Pietrelcina, San Giovanni Rotondo (FG) 2013, p. 220.

45. Ibid. With Padre Ignazio, who was the guardian of the convent of San Giovanni Rotondo from September 10, 1922 to August 25, 1925, regarding the groundlessness of the calumny, in agreement are Padre Paolino da Casacalenda (in *Le mie memorie intorno a Padre Pio*, Gerardo Di Flumeri (Ed.), Edizioni Padre Pio da Pietrelcina, San Giovanni Rotondo 1978, pp. 192-193), Padre Agostino da San Marco in Lamis (in his *Diario*, Edizioni Padre Pio da Pietrelcina, San Giovanni Rotondo 2012, p. 285 and ff.), Padre Lorenzo da San Marco in Lamis (Cf. *Positio super virtutibus*, op. cit., vol. III/1, p. 363) and Padre Raffaele da Sant'Elia a Pianisi (Cf. G. Di Flumeri, *Il Beato Padre Pio*, op. cit., p. 414).

46. F. Spaccucci, *I cinque Papi di Padre Pio*, op. cit., p. 51.

47. F. Peloso, *Don Luigi Orione e Padre Pio da Pietrelcina*, Jaca Book, Milan 1998, p. 45.

48. Ibid, p. 56.

49. *Positio super virtutibus*, op. cit., vol. I/1, p. 128.

50. Cf. G. Di Flumeri, *Il Beato Padre Pio*, op. cit., pp. 42 and ff.

51. Ibid, p. 414.

52. *Positio super virtutibus*, op. cit., vol. IV, section I, p. 65.

53. M. Crovini, *Relazione*, op. cit., attachment 10, p. 14.

54. *Positio super virtutibus*, op. cit., vol. IV, section I, p. 69.

55. M. Crovini, *Relazione*, op. cit., p. 16.

56. "Letter of Father General Clemente da Milwaukee to the Holy Father John XXIII," in *Positio super virtutibus*, op. cit., vol. IV, section I, p. 447. It was Father Amedeo Fabrocini, provincial minister of the Province of

Capuchin Friars Minor of Foggia, who suggested to the Minister General to ask for an apostolic visit, to shed light on some "rumors that in San Giovanni Rotondo accused my confreres of undue appropriations of sums destined to the Casa Sollievo della Sofferenza [...] convinced [...] of the innocence of my confreres [...] to discredit any gossip and to offer an objective proof to my convictions" ("Testimony of Padre Amedeo Fabrocini," in *Positio super virtutibus*, op. cit., vol. II, p. 29).

57. "Letter of Father General Clemente da Milwaukee to the Holy Father John XXIII," in *Positio super virtutibus*, op. cit., vol. IV, section I, p. 447.

58. "Attachment to the letter of Padre General Clemente da Milwaukee to the Holy Father John XXIII," in ibid, p. 448.

59. Ibid.

60. G. Di Flumeri, A. da Ripabottoni, "The visit of Monsignor Maccari," in *Positio super virtutibus*, op. cit., vol. IV, section I, p. 99.

61. M. Crovini, "Relazione," op. cit., p. 17.

62. Ibid. Evidently, Don Umberto Terenzi referred to Monsignor Bontempi and not (as it has been wrongly interpreted) to Monsignor Maccari when, on June 15, 1960 he wrote to Padre Daniele da Roma: "For matters regarding Padre Pio I can assure you that the Visitor has already been named who is not Mons. Ronca, but another Monsignor from Rome, my fellow student in the Seminario Romano, an excellent friend of mine and a very righteous and 'easily guided' person." (F. Chiocci, L. Cirri, *Padre Pio. Storia di una vittima*, op. cit., vol. III, p. 508). In fact, Monsignor Maccari was chosen on July 13, after the refusal of Monsignor Bontempi, expressed on June 28 (Cf. *infra*).

63. Padre Giustino Gaballo da Lecce and Fra Masseo Cannito da San Martino in Pensilis.

64. Cf. A. da Ripabottoni, "Le registrazioni," in *Positio super virtutibus*, op. cit., vol. IV, section I, pp. 490 and ff.

65. For more detailed information regarding this occurrence, we advise the reading of: S. Campanella, *Obœdientia et Pax. La vera storia di una falsa persecuzione*, LEV – Edizioni Padre Pio da Pietrelcina, Roma – San Giovanni Rotondo (FG) 2011, pp. 111 and ff.

66. Cf. "Pro-memoria of S. E. Monsignor Valentino Vailati of October 16 and 17, 1984 after a conversation with Monsignor Loris Francesco Capovilla," in *Positio super virtutibus*, op. cit., vol. I/1, p. 137.

67. In the *Annuario Pontificio* Monsignor Maccari "is listed as the Secretary of the Vicariate of Rome, of the Office for Divine Cult, the Ap-

ostolic Visit, the discipline of the Clergy and of the Christian people and consultor of the Congregation of the Council " (Cf. *Positio super virtutibus*, op. cit., vol. IV, p. 324). But, always within the Vicariate, he was part of the Diocesan Catechetical Commission and of the Work of Eccesiastical Vocations and of the regular clergy (Cf. *Annuario Pontificio*, year 1961, Tipografia Poliglotta Vaticana, pp. 1067-1068). Moreover, he was Domestic Prelate of His Holiness and consultor of the Congregation of the Council (Cf. ibid, pp. 943 and 1203).

68.   John XXIII, *Pater amabilis. Agende del Pontefice, 1958 – 1963*, critical edition, Mauro Velati (Ed.), Istituto per le Scienze Religiose "Giovanni XXIII," Bologna 2007, p. 139.

69.   C. Maccari, "Relazione al Cardinale Joseph Ratzinger," in *Positio super virtutibus*, op. cit., vol. IV, section I, p. 424.

70.   Ibid, p. 426.

71.   C. Maccari, "Relazione della visita apostolica," in *Beatificationis et Canonizationis Servi Dei Pii a Pietrelcina. Positio super virtutibus*, vol. IV-A, Bari, Tipografia Favia, 1997, p. 18.

72.   C. Maccari, "Relazione al Cardinale Joseph Ratzinger," in *Positio super virtutibus*, op. cit., vol. IV, section I, p. 425.

73.   Cf. John XXIII, *Pater amabilis*, op. cit., pp. 289 and 361.

74.   "Pro-memoria of S. E. Monsignor Valentino Vailati of October 16 and 17, 1984 after a conversation with Monsignor Loris Francesco Capovilla," in *Positio super virtutibus*, op. cit., vol. I/1, p. 137.

75.   L.F. Capovilla, "Arcivescovo Carlo Maccari (1913 – 1997)," note for the Vaticanist of *Avvenire* Mimmo Muolo, ds, April 18, 1997.

76.   "Testimony of Padre Amedeo Fabrocini," in *Positio super virtutibus*, op. cit., vol. II, p. 29. Padre Bonaventura was able to inform with more anticipation Padre Amedeo because Monsignor Maccari communicated to him only in July 29 that he would have had "to make known only to the Provincial Minister of Foggia that the following day, July 30, he would be arrIving in Foggia straight to San Giovanni Rotondo" (Bonaventura da Pavullo, "Visita apostolica di Mons. Carlo Maccari a San Giovanni Rotondo," in *Positio super virtutibus*, op. cit., vol. IV, section I, p. 324).

77.   C. Maccari, "Relazione della visita apostolica," in *Positio super virtutibus*, op. cit., vol. IV-A, p. 19.

78.   "Testimony of Padre Amedeo Fabrocini," in *Positio super virtutibus*, op. cit., vol. II, p. 30.

79. We are certain about the start of the visit, but about its last day the various sources do not agree.
80. "Letter of S. E. Monsignor Carlo Maccari (archbishop of Ancona) to a non-specified 'monsignor' of the Congregation for the Doctrine of the Faith," November 6, 1974, ds, *Archives of the Congregation for the Doctrine of the Faith*, 255/19, fg. 2.
81. Ibid, fg. 3.
82. C. Maccari, "I miei incontri con X," in *Positio super virtutibus*, op. cit., vol. IVA, p. 133. It is not a circumstantial answer to clear himself.
    Padre Eusebio Notte, who was the personal assistant of Padre Pio, took advantage of the confidence that had been established with him to ask him: "Padre, but why not leave these pious women alone... So many spread the gossip that goes around!" And the elderly confrere, becoming serious, answered him: "My son, but what would happen to them?" (cf. "Testimony of Padre Eusebio Notte," in *Positio super virtutibus*, op. cit., vol. II, p. 296). This conversation taking place in an atmosphere of familiarity and in a context beyond suspicion, shows that effectively the priority interest behind the words and the attitude of Padre Pio was the salvation of souls (Cf. also *below* 3.4).
83. C. Maccari, "I miei incontri con X," in *Positio super virtutibus*, op. cit., vol. IV-A, p. 135.
84. C. Maccari, "Relazione della visita apostolica," in *Positio super virtutibus*, op. cit., vol. IV-A, p. 81.
85. "Testimony of Padre Amedeo Fabrocini," in *Positio super virtutibus*, op. cit., vol. II, p. 30.
86. "Testimony of Padre Carmelo Durante," in ibid, p. 809.
87. "Testimony of Professor Francesco Lotti," in ibid, p. 1238.
88. "Testimony of Professor Giuseppe Sala," in ibid, p. 741
89. "Testimony of Rev. Giosuè Fini," in ibid, p. 1307. In agreement with this opinion are many other witnesses (Cf. *Positio super virtutibus*, op. cit., vol. IV, pp. 193, 197, 208, 210, 216, 222, 231).
90. R. D'Addario, "Brevi cenni riguardanti la Vita del P. Pio e la mia lunga dimora con lui," in M. Iasenzaniro, *Padre Pio. Profilo di un santo*, Edizioni Padre Pio da Pietrelcina, San Giovanni Rotondo (FG) 2009, vol. II, p. 409.
91. John XXIII, *Pater amabilis*, op. cit., p. 160.
92. C. Maccari, "Relazione della visita apostolica," in *Positio super virtutibus*, op. cit., vol. IV-A, p. 90.

93. Ibid, p. 103. The phrases in quotation marks are of one of the witnesses interrogated by Monsignor Maccari.
94. Ibid, p. 93.
95. Ibid, p. 94.
96. Cf. ibid, p. 101.
97. Cf. ibid, p. 102.
98. Cf. G. Gigliozzi, …*E Padre Pio mi disse…*, op. cit., p. 119.
99. Cf. G.A. Pezzati, "La morte di Monsignor Carlo Maccari," in *Voce di Padre Pio*, n. 6, June 1998, p. 17. The source of the author is the secretary of Monsignor Maccari, Don Almerino Quercetti, who has validated, with a brief writing in the same page, the story of Pezzati.
100. M. Morra, *Padre Pio e la Chiesa madre di santi e di peccatori*, Edizioni Casa Sollievo della Sofferenza – Edizioni Padre Pio da Pietrelcina, San Giovanni Rotondo (FG) 2007, p. 337.
101. M. Muolo, "Maccari, un vescovo di prima linea," in *Avvenire*, April 19, 1997, p. 7.
102. Cf. C. Maccari, "Relazione della visita apostolica," in *Positio super virtutibus*, op. cit., vol. IV-A, p. 81.
103. Cf. ibid, p. 86.
104. Ibid, p. 85.
105. Ibid, p. 86.
106. Cf. ibid.
107. Ibid.
108. Cf. ibid, pp. 85-86. n. 145.
109. P. Philippe, "Report and vote of February 8, 1969," ds, *Archivio della Congregazione per la Dottrina della Fede*, 255/19, p. 4. With the judgment expressed by Archbishop Philippe other sources are in agreement: "Results of the investigation made by M. R. P. Rosario Borraccino, Provincial Minister of the Capuchin Friars Minor of Foggia, answering prayers addressed to him by the archbishop of Manfredonia, His Excellency Most Rev. Mons. Valentino Vailati," June 13, 1972, attachment n. 14, in M. Crovini, "Report," op. cit.; the "Testimony of Padre Alberto D'Apolito," in *Positio super virtutibus*, op. cit., vol. II, p. 72; the "Testimony of ins. Maria Pennisi," in ibid, p. 118; the "Testimony of Padre Amedeo Fabrocini," in ibid, p. 14; the "Testimony of Padre Carmelo Durante," in ibid, pp. 831 and ff.; the "Testimony of Maria Grazia Massa," in ibid, pp. 1586 and ff.; the "Testimony of Girolama Longo," in ibid, p. 1596.

110. Cf. S. Campanella, *Obœdientia et pax. La vera storia di una falsa persecuzione*, op. cit., pp. 183 and ff.
111. Cf. C. Maccari, "Relazione della visita apostolica," in *Positio super virtutibus*, op. cit., vol. IV-A, p. 85.
112. "Testimony of Nina Campanile," in *Positio super virtutibus*, op. cit., vol. II, p. 1652. From the same testimony we learn the motive which induced Padre Pio to dedicate greater attention to some of his spiritual daughters with respect to others: "To some weak soul, which did not support the strong way and went away from the route undertaken for the conquest of perfection, Padre Pio tossed into the air a metaphor: 'Fish swim toward the hook, attracted by the bait; without this, they go away.' Then the soul understood and swiftly swam toward the hook without the bait. But he did not act in this way with strong and already tried souls. He made them run on ascending roads of sacrifice upon sacrifice, following his example. [...] And this is the motive why among all his spiritual daughters the Padre took care of somebody in a particular way; but it is not always the same soul. And such a soul was not among those more dedicated to sacrifice, more among the weaker and imperfect. He put himself at the disposal of such souls with the evangelical spirit of service, following the example of the Master who came to serve and not to be served. And in this sense he could say to the souls, as more than once he said to me: 'Each one of your desires is a command for me'; and he acted as a matter of consequence" (Ibid, p. 1646). The testimony of Nina Campanile is particularly important inasmuch as she has personally experienced, although in a different way, the sentiment of jealousy for having been the first to be "treated in an exceptional manner above the other spiritual sisters," deluding herself to be the object "of special predilection of the Padre and even of God," to then be placed in the second line when "other souls" took her place (Cf. ibid). About it, therefore, this spiritual daughter of the stigmatized Capuchin has testified: "Padre Pio has used special preference toward a soul over all the others, always in the range of spiritual direction, for the acquisition of Christian perfection, as he has done first with me, then (the soul was not always the same) for [Martha] and finally for Cleonice Morcaldi. It must be said, however, that Padre Pio, notwithstanding this method, did not exclude any other soul from his pastoral cares. [...] Late in 1917 I noticed

that Padre Pio started to change method in directing me, showing himself to be like a mother. I became aware of it and asked for the reason and he answered me: 'The nature of your soul is that of a baby girl; and as a baby girl I must treat you.' And I must recognize you to have remained, in relation to God, always a baby girl […]. Until 1920 through a particular commitment Padre Pio tried to make me grow in the way of the spirit and then gradually he put me in line with the others. I did not succeed in accepting always the will of God and once in a while I failed in the face of the trials to which the Padre subjected me; and therefore misunderstandings and rebellions on my part were born. […] When in fact Padre Pio began to direct spiritually [Martha and her sisters] – in a particular way [Martha] – and I in some certain way believed myself to be relegated to second place, I felt seized by a strong resentment of jealousy which, augmented by precarious conditions of health, provoked a true rupture between me and the Padre: I arrived until not believing anymore in his sanctity. But in the bottom of my heart there remained always a sentiment of esteem and filial love toward him, so that I made a prayer to the Lord to give me a sign of the sanctity of the Padre, by sending me even a heavy malady. The Lord took me at my word and on July 26, 1924 I got seriously sick, remaining in coma for several days. Subsequently I recovered, but that terrible malady I carried with me for about two years. […] In a letter Padre Pio had foretold for me the terrible trial which I would be meeting; but at that time I did not understand what it was all about. During the trial Padre Pio helped me in every way: through advice, prayer and through letters that he sent me when, for health reasons, I left San Giovanni Rotondo. Thus, through the grace of God and the help of the Padre, I overcame the terrible trial and did not doubt anymore of the sanctity of Padre Pio" (Ibid, pp. 1649 and ff.).

113. M. Iasenzaniro, *Padre Pio. Profilo di un santo*, op. cit., vol. II, pp. 41 and ff.

114. "Testimony of Padre Carmelo Durante," in *Positio super virtutibus*, op. cit., vol. II, p. 836.

Chapter IV

THE "SOCIAL" MERCY OF PADRE PIO

The mercy by which Padre Pio was the instrument of the Divine will is shown in his attention to the essential needs, including the earthly, of the men and women of his time. Everyone knows the most significant work that he realized, the hospital "Casa Sollievo della Sofferenza," but few know that this was preceded by another hospital and was followed by still other initiatives aimed at providing the population of San Giovanni Rotondo and neighboring areas adequate religious education, personal and professional, especially during the years of economic and social deterioration immediately following the Second World War.

Some of these activities still offer their services today, while others have long since exhausted their task for a variety of reasons, but remaining always valid are the benefits they have sown during the years in which they operated and the example of attention to the concrete needs of individuals that often restrict the dignity of the human person.

"San Francesco" Hospital

Beginning with March 26, 1914 Padre Pio harbored deep in his soul a sentiment of "compassion for the miseries of others" and was determined to do anything "in the Lord" to free from their ills any afflicted person "whether in soul or in body." He would have even been willing to take upon himself "all their afflictions, yielding in his or her favor the fruits of such sufferings," just to save them from the trial. It was, for him, a new sensation. He considered it "a very special favor of God," considering that in the past he had felt "naturally little or no piety" for the needs of others.[1]

For a few years, however, his charitable efforts were carried on through his personal help on a case-by-case basis. After the news spread of his permanent stigmatization, that possibility was completely changed. The grapevine revealed itself quickly as a formidable vehicle of diffusion, so much so that the first brief article, unsigned, published by *Il Giornale d'Italia* about eight months after September 20, 1918, testified that "the common people are attracted to the convent to visit the 'Santo.'"[2] Even more explicitly, six days later, the weekly magazine of Capitanata, *Il Foglietto*, stated that "many faithful [...] from all parts of the peninsula are coming to him trusting in his God-given superhuman powers."[3]

On the wave of his popularity, amplified by the articles in the press, the pilgrimage phenomenon grew, so much so that, on June 19, 1920, the Capuchin who lived in San Giovanni Rotondo made the news in the British newspaper *Daily Mail* which informed its readers that "people are witnessing extraordinary scenes in Foggia[4] every day [...]. Long lines appear before the young Franciscan and look with astonishment at the marks on his hands, sandal covered feet and head. These signs have been authenticated from a medical point of view and it is said that they correspond in detail to the marks left on the Crucified One of Nazareth."[5]

Many of these pilgrims, with the prospect of obtaining a miracle through the intercession of this religious privileged by the Lord, would leave religious offerings, even substantial ones, in his wounded hands.[6] With this availability Padre Pio could do much more for the wretched, towards whom he felt compassion.

But he was bound by a vow of poverty. Because of this he wrote to his Provincial Minister, Padre Benedetto da San Marco in Lamis, and asked him:

"If a sum of money were presented to us religious by a secular person with the express will of the same that it be used as judged best in conscience for the greatest good, for the glory of God and for relief of others, is it contrary to our rule of life if the religious to whom is presented said offerings in these terms, were to take such an offering and use it as he sees fit and so judges in conscience?"[7]

In return, Padre Benedetto answered:

"It is licit to distribute to the poor the offerings received for such purpose, because in doing so we simply execute the will of the givers and in no way do we exercise dominion. It would be imputable to receive money without the givers expressing in any way the purpose; but when they determine its use, even in a disjointed way, then there is no offense to our duties, because it is to be used as they desire."[8]

The first need that presented itself in the eyes of the stigma-tized Capuchin was the sanitary one. Many of those who turned to him to ask for his prayers, in fact, were either sick themselves or relatives of sick persons. The old hospital of San Giovanni

Rotondo, built in the 13th century, was closed at the beginning of 1900 and, from that moment on, there was not in the town "even an outpatient clinic, for the most needed medications."[9] Diseases like smallpox, tuberculosis and pellagra were very widespread. Cases of blood poisoning were not rare.[10] Because of the living conditions of the population, contagion took place easily and often infections had a fatal outcome, in part because "the few doctors" who lived in the place, "although animated by a high spirit of altruism and animated by a profound dedication to sacrifice," were forced to exercise their profession in less than ideal conditions and sometimes had to perform "operations, even delicate ones, in the 'house' of the patients themselves."[11]

Those who had "need of surgery" were "forced to travel to Foggia or Naples." The population had long since noted "the lack of a hospital worthy of a civilized city." Professor Adelchi Fabrocini, President of the local Congregation of Charity, was already working on trying to obtain "through many private subsidies" to reach that goal. His was an ambitious project, which foresaw "an operating room, well furnished and equipped with the principal surgical instruments for every kind of operation; an outpatient clinic and two wards capable of five beds each, on the first floor; two rooms for the accommodation of the infirmarians, two rooms for the administrative offices of the same and two rooms for sick people who would not want to stay in the common ward, but wanted to be independent, in the second floor." After having obtained its disposal on the part of the Municipality, Prof. Fabrocini started to adapt for use the "dilapidated edifice of the former Monte Frumentario" near the old hospital, where at one time were deposited the surpluses of grain.[12] Rumors of the initiative reached the convent and Padre Pio decided to do his part. But it was the Superior of the Friary,

Padre Ignazio da Ielsi, who in his place took care of the practical aspects of the initiative as a member of the Committee for erecting the hospital.

The chosen real estate, however, after an attentive analysis, revealed itself to be unfit because it lacked a "garden, salt, water, cesspools, mortuary room and locales for service personnel." The new President of the Congregation, Doctor Leandro Giuva, "after considering that the founder, Padre Pio da Pietrelcina, in various conversations, even with disinterested persons, skilled or technical, accepted their opinion: that the place where the hospital could be adapted and which is absolutely incomparable with that of the 'Monte' locale is the former convent of the Poor Clares [...] and for this reason he has given the broadest assurances to increase the sum of L. 50,000 to re-adapt a part of the former convent of the Poor Clares." In the meeting dated August 6, 1922 the "proposal to invite the autonomous Commission for the hospital to urgently meet again [...] with the intent of coming to a solution, which might satisfy fully the needs of the town"[13] was submitted "to a secret vote." In that gathering the Congregation did not approve any solution, but voted to return to the subject matter on October 29.

This time Giuva forcefully presented the strong orientation of the Committee regarding the construction of the hospital, which "ended in determining to suspend the present work and proceed to negotiate with this administration," recognizing "that those buildings, though renovated, could never meet even the most modest needs of a place of care." He therefore formulated this proposal: "To register it in perpetuity to a person to be named by the representative of the donors, Padre Ignazio Testa da Ielsi, Guardian of the Capuchin convent, for the purpose of instituting a work of charity, the entire edifice of the 'Monte'

[…] with an annual fee of Lire 600, deposited 50 thousand Lire in the postal savings bank (Casa di Risparmio) on behalf of the President of the Congregation of Charity, for the adaptation of the former convent of the Poor Clares." In addition, following the vote, which gave the green light to the exchange, the Congregation approved "that the projected work be drawn up and the bidding of contracts be announced, in in accord with the laws."[14] On January 3 the decision was ratified by the Commission, which met "under the presidency of the Prefect Commissioner Cav. Uff. Michele Nigri" and decided to "acknowledge unsuitable for the local hospital said site of the 'Monte' such that continuation of the work underway be renounced" and determined to give rise to the hospital in the convent of the Poor Clares, with separate entrance on the western side, readapting the existing premises and constructing the operating room, a new ward and other rooms on available soil to the south."[15]

At the end of the year "the work around the hospital was almost fully booked" and Dr. Giuva, "wishing to offer a token of gratitude to Rev.mo Padre Pio da Pietralcina [sic] and the Capuchin order, to which he belongs, proposes […] calling a part of this Congregation of Charity the Rev. Padre Pio da Pietrelcina [sic], with the faculty to be its representative himself or through another person, and to transmit this right to the Superior pro-tempore who will be holding this office in the convent of San Giovanni Rotondo in the future" and "to confer this right for good in perpetuity, functioning as the hospital's chaplain to a religious from the convent of Capuchins in this city, appointed by the Superior of said convent."[16]

A few months later some "rumors" spread in town that "the new hospital will be called the Civil Hospital of St. Francis". Two members of the Congregation, Federico Fiorentino and Mateo

Squarcella, at its meeting of July 10, 1924, "asked the President if the rumors were true." Dr. Leandro Giuva confirmed them and explained that the Capuchin Fathers, in keeping with their vow of humility as sons and followers of St. Francis, did not want to see a confrere of theirs while still living be given the name of a Hospital." But "these confreres of the reverend friars did not find the reasons to be just, and they insist, out of a sense of gratitude and esteem, that the new hospital should have the name: Civil Hospital of Padre Pio da Pietralcina [sic], precisely to show to the benefactors and contributors that their money entrusted to the holy man was not misdirected, but spent and dedicated to the construction of a hospital which, through the work and intercession of this pious and humble little Friar of Assisi [sic] will welcome so many unhappy poor persons, who in their turn, will also bless the fruitful and charitable hand of the founder Padre Pio. The Congregation in its deliberations unanimously found the proposal of the members Fiorentino and Squarcella, recognizing all the merits of the aforesaid Padre Pio" decided that the hospital be named: Civil Hospital of Padre Pio da Pietralcina [sic]."[17] Eventually the common sense and orientation of the friars prevailed.

The thus exaggerated expression of gratitude was due to the fact that the contribution of the stigmatized Capuchin was not limited to just the 50,000 lire poured out in the work of refurbishing and adapting the former convent of the Poor Clares. In fact the furnishing and equipment necessary for the medical activities was provided by benefactors who esteemed Padre Pio.[18]

On April 23, 1925, finally, the hospital dedicated to St. Francis was inaugurated. It was divided into two wards, one for men and one for women, with seven beds each. There were also two rooms reserved, for a total of twenty places. It had already been established in advance that, for the poor, care had to be given free.[19] The direction of the clinic was entrusted to Doctor Francescantonio Giuva. As vice-director, Doctor Angelo Maria Merla was nominated.[20] The administrative organization, presided over by Doctor Leandro Giuva as President pro tempore of the Congregation, was made up of the Mayor Francesco Morcaldi and by two spiritual daughters of Padre Pio: Vittoria Ventrella and Angela Serritelli.[21] Assistance in the infirmary was entrusted to the Suore Apostole del Sacro Cuore di Gesù[22] until 1920 and, from the first of September 1928 on, to the Adoratrici del Sangue di Cristo.[23] For the most delicate surgical interventions, Doctor Francesco Paolo Bucci, serving at the Ospedali Riuniti[24] came from Foggia twice a week.

At first everything went smoothly and a part of the offerings coming to Padre Pio contributed regularly to the current expenses of the healthcare activities. Within a few years, however, there arose the first problems in administrative management, which resulted in a dispute between various entities and an "anonymous" contributor to the Prefecture of Foggia. The Mayor, Antonio Bramante, noticed that the "masonry work on the civic hospital" was on course and wrote a letter to the President of the Congregation to remind him "that the environs are the property of the municipality; and hence no modifications were to be deployed without the consent of this Administration" and to ask him "to immediately suspend any such work."[25] Two days later, Bramante also sent a letter to the mason Michele Centra enjoining him to suspend at once the execution of the work."[26] Within a few days, Dr. Leandro Giuva replied to the Mayor disputing his arguments and stating that "the premises of the Hospital virtually and also legally belong to the Congregation of Charity starting with the day they were ceded by this Administration to erect the hospital there." The President also stressed that the Congregation was running the hospital "in a most commendable way, especially given the limited financial resources at its disposal, without any interference on the part of this Municipality, which has consistently refused even the most dutiful contribution"; for this reason he judged "absolutely inappropriate" the intervention of the Mayor "regarding jobs." Moreover he felt compelled to point out that: "the urgency of the work did not allow any delay of time, as would have been necessary if it had to resort to a contract with bidding"; that the mason responsible "has the undeniable ability to execute the work" and "has shown the absolute impossibility of reducing prices if one wants to pretend that the work should meet all the requirements for which they were contracted." And, to prove it, he attached to the letter the signed contract and the budget of the architect.[27]

The matter was complicated by the sending of an anonymous complaint to the "Royal Prefecture of Capitanata" according to which "the President of the local Congregation of Charity would have contracted privately for L. 4,000 without seeking public bids."[28] The Prefect asked for clarifications from the Mayor, who confirmed the denunciation, specifying that, actually, "the amount" of the works was for "L. 5,000" and ensuring that he had already "invited Dr. Giuva to suspend the masonry work underway on the premises of the Civic Hospital since those premises are owned by this municipality."[29]

Both the anonymous complaint and the tenor of the answer of the President of the Congregation to the Mayor, above all the not so veiled accusation to the Municipality of refusing "even the most dutiful contribution " to the Civic Hospital "Saint Francis" clearly allows us to guess the social and economic difficulties in which the initiative continued to find itself.

The Congregation, in fact, starting from the first months of the new charitable activity for the sick, "although it had sensibly bettered its patrimonial revenue, could not cover the financial needs that are necessary to maintain the Hospital, whose needs are multiplying (due, more than anything else, to the continuous requests for free admission from poor citizens),"[30] notwithstanding that "the medical personnel did not create any burden as to expenses for the Congregation inasmuch as it lent its work free in favor of the poor."[31] That is why, as early as 1934, there was a cash deficit of L. 7,350 lire.[32]

To these criticisms of the economic order were probably added the consequences of the injuries provoked by two successive earthquakes, although they were not very strong, that occurred in the province of Foggia in 1937. The strongest one, on July 17 at 5 p.m., numbered 7 in the Mercalli scale (5.07 in the Richter scale) with the epicenter in San Severo, which in San Giovanni Rotondo had an intensity equal to 5 in the Mercalli scale; the second, on December 15 at 9 p.m., numbered 5-6 in the Mercalli scale (4.72 in the Richter scale) with the epicenter in San Paolo di Civitate, had an intensity of 2 in the Mercalli scale in San Giovanni Rotondo.[33] It is possible, therefore, that the hospital building may have been damaged due to the earthquakes, above all due to the first quake,[34] whose effects could have been aggravated by the second. Due to carelessness, or lack of funds, or not to interrupt the service no restructuring was done.

The fact is that, at the beginning of 1940, the structure was still providing its service, even if it went "forward haltingly."[35] On the eve of the Epiphany, in fact, the new President of the hospital, engineer Antonio Campanile, as usual, knocked at the door of the convent to collect the contribution of the Capuchins. Opening the door to him was the Guardian,

Padre Raffaele da Sant'Elia a Pianisi, who treated him coldly and, bluntly said to him: "You remember the convent only when you come to ask for offerings. In the contract there is the specification that the Superior of the convent is also a member of the Commission and the Council. Have you ever called me in so many years?" The President, surprised, astounded and a bit offended, tried to apologize as best he could. Padre Raffaele at any rate gave him the offering, but the atmosphere remained tense.[36]

That same evening, after dinner, four friars found themselves in room #13 for recreation. Padre Pio was there as were two of the original friars of San Giovanni Rotondo, Padre Eusebio and Padre Leo, along with Padre Raffaele. The Guardian had a weight on his conscience from which he had to break free and, with great embarrassment, went right to the subject: "Padre Pio, I really did it today." Then he told him what had happened in the morning. The stigmatized Capuchin pretended not to hear. He kept praying with the Rosary beads in his hand, shaking his head slightly to the left and right. Emboldened by the silence of his confrere, Padre Raffaele went further and suggested: "Why don't we build a hospital here, with at least a hundred beds?" The proposal caught the attention of Padre Pio who, at this point, intervened in the discussion by asking: "Where?" "On the land of Maria Basilio," the Guardian replied, referring to a State-owned plot located a few dozen meters from the convent[37], granted to the Mayor, Antonio Bramante, for the realization of a charitable work, by a young woman from Turin, who became a spiritual daughter of the charismatic friar and moved to San Giovanni Rotondo. Padre Pio opened his eyes. He seemed to be looking into the void, while saying: "*Ce li ma fa*: We must do it."[38]

"Casa Sollievo della Sofferenza"

When Padre Pio replied "*Ce li ma fa,*" his eyes seemed to be looking far off. He quickly made his own the proposal and began to talk about it to an agronomist of Perugia, Mario Sanvico, and to a blind man who had lost his sight as a child, Pietro Cugino.

This "desire of the Capuchin" quickly became known and was an object of attention among his spiritual sons who began immediately to make it happen. Already in the afternoon of January 9, in a prefabricated cottage shared by Sanvico and the district doctor in the zone of Mugello, Guglielmo Sanguinetti, both of whom had moved to San Giovanni Rotondo to Padre Pio, the following met: "Miss Ida Seitz, Doctor Carlo Kisvarday, Doctor Mario Sanvico, Mrs. Maria Antonietta Sanvico, and Mrs. Mary Kisvarday came together to form a Committee for the foundation of a clinic according to the intentions of Padre Pio of Pietrelcina. […] The Committee was composed as follow: the founder of the work: Padre Pio of Pietrelcina (who at the moment did not wish to be named); Secretary: Dr. Mario Sanvico; Cashier and Bookkeeper: Dr. Carlo Kisvarday; Medical technician: Dr. Guglielmo Sanguinetti; Director of the internal organization: Miss Ida Seitz. It was agreed that everything before being implemented will have to be submitted to the advice of Padre Pio."[39]

After the meeting, Sanvico and Kisvarday reached Padre Pio in his cell and showed him the proposal. The friar was excited and said, "My great work on this earth begins this evening. I bless you (Sanvico and Kisvarday on their knees) and all who will contribute to my work, which promises to be ever bigger and greater." Then, taking from his pocket "a golden marengo equivalent to ten francs" that he had received that morning from a devotee, he added: "I too want to offer my mite!…"[40] That same evening the cashier, Dr. Kisvarday, was able to note in the register of contributions, all in all, 10 gold francs and 967 lire.[41]

It was the same Padre Pio, at a distance of some days, on the evening of Sunday January 14, who indicated the name of the clinic to be erected as: "Casa Sollievo della Sofferenza."[42] Even the eyes of the members of the committee looked into the future. The Saint Francis Hospital, in fact, already in difficulty "due to the laziness or lack of trust" of the men who "did not know how to be at the height of the initiative" and who "did not commit themselves as they should have done,"[43] almost certainly received the final blow from a series of "alluvial rains"[44] that devastated the province of Foggia from January 10, 1940 to the end of the same month.[45] Perhaps because of some crack going back to the two earthquakes of 1937 made deeper "both due to lack of maintenance or to a defect of the original construction" and above all to the "seepings of water in a part of the environment [...] the substructure of a pavement covering the ground floor of the terrace has crumbled and numerous fissures have been verified along the separating perimeter walls; a fissure corresponding to the northeast corner of the building meanwhile has created a frightening overhang such as to force the Authority to close the Hospital."[46]

It has not been possible to provide certain data about this collapse and the consequent closure of the structure which, however, should have taken place before August 24, 1940, the day during which a deliberation of the Mayor was approved, with which he authorized the liquidation of the "expenses of construction, the distribution and supply of surgical instruments for the Municipality's outpatient clinic for the poor," evidently meant to meet the cost of the service of sanitary assistance that the laws in force of the time and the Ministry of the Interior held obligatory for "all the Municipalities where other institutions do not provide it."[47]

The Second World War slowed down, but did not stop, the realization of that idea.[48] However, one had to wait until October 5, 1946 for the first official step: the constitution, in the presence of the notary Girolamo Gaggianelli of Foggia, of Company Shares in the "'Casa Sollievo della Sofferenza'" (Hospital Clinic) in San Giovanni Rotondo (Foggia)," for the purpose of constructing "a Hospital Clinic destined for the cure and assistance of the sick even spiritually."[49] The society had a capital of a thousand shares of a thousand lire each, equivalent to a million. The shares were distributed among the faithful who were closest to Padre Pio[50] with the formal commitment that they would have renounced any profit.[51]

Barely four days later, Maria Basilio made available to the Society the terrain which she had obtained as a concession. The following morning the Serritelli family of San Giovanni Rotondo gave another strip of land adjacent to the preceding.

Thus, on May 16, 1947, with a simple ceremony Padre Pio blessed the first stone of the future large hospital. On the 19th, about twenty workers, without even a preliminary plan, started the excavation for the construction of the road leading to the site. In the coffers there were barely four million and a half lire, but the friar of Pietrelcina had wanted at all costs the immediate start of the work.[52] To this objective he held for almost two years in San Giovanni Rotondo Don Peppino Orlando, his long-time friend and townmate, named delegate councilor of the society,[53] and "every evening" he pushed him: "Have you understood that you must start the works?" "My Piuccio," the priest answered, "why should people laugh behind my and your back? Starting the works for a big clinic without a plan, without a design, without an architect?" But Padre Pio did not want to listen to reasonings and insisted: "You must start the works." At the end Don Peppino gave up:

> "One evening, just to satisfy him, I said to him: 'Piuccio, tomorrow I shall make a road in those rocks donated by Maria Basilio; pay attention, however, it's only a road that I know how to make.' Of course, but exactly the road: I bought two balls of twine and with 20 workers I started the road 4 meters wide, aligning with the stretched twine two small dry walls using rocks that I extracted from the rocky soil.
> Padre Pio spied every day from the window of the convent and in the evening he brushed from my cassock the dust that had fallen on it during the works of the day. How happy he was!"[54]

Looking at those pioneers with human eyes, their enterprise seemed to be foolhardiness, so much so that they were described as, without half terms, "crazy megalomaniacs."[55] But Padre Pio looked at his Work with the eyes of faith and charity.

His trust in Providence was soon repaid. A noted English journalist of the prestigious weekly *The Economist*, Barbara Ward, a Catholic, in Italy for an investigation regarding the post-war reconstruction, made a stop at San Giovanni Rotondo to ask from the now famous Capuchin prayer for the conversion of her Protestant fiancé, the Australian Robert Jackson, delegate adviser of UNRRA,[56] in charge of the aids of UNO in Europe, Africa and in the Far East. Padre Pio answered her: "Yes, if the Lord wants, he will be converted." Not much satisfied with the answer, she replied: "But, Padre, and when?" "If the Lord wants, even now," the Capuchin closed the discourse. And precisely when Miss Ward talked with Padre Pio, in London her future spouse was being baptized in a Catholic church.

All this happened in the autumn of 1947, a few days after the start of the works of excavation. Made curious and interested by that project, the English journalist would, later on, pressure her husband to have a contribution from UNRRA recognized for the "Casa Sollievo della Sofferenza"[57] to be erected.

The idea of the donation was supported as an homage in memory of the former mayor of New York Fiorello La Guardia, who had also been director general of the same international organization, whose family originally came from the province of Foggia.[58] 400 million lire were allocated, a large sum for the period.[59] When, however, the paperwork was formalized with the sending to the American agency AUSA, on the part of the Administration International Aids of the Italian Government of the list of the works to be financed in Italy, without explanation[60] the request for the "Casa Sollievo della Sofferenza" was reduced to 252 million, with the prospect of receiving only 100 million.[61] At the end, the contribution allocated, with the approval of the Italian Government, was 250 million.[62]

In order to be able to go ahead in the works of the hospital, besides money, there was also need of an executive project for the building. On October 10, 1940 Padre Pio called architect Sirio Giametta of Frattamaggiore, of the province of Naples, and he asked him to design a hospital "where a sick person feels that it is his home: a comfortable place, full of light, and very homey."[63] One month after the project was already done.[64] Before starting its realization, in July 1946, "in the convent a commission of technicians and friends of Padre Pio gathered […]. Taking part there were two Roman noblemen, the Marchesi Sacchetti and Patrizi, Doctor Di Giacomo, a benefactor and friend of the Padre, and a technician, the architect Siviero di Roma." From the meeting it was determined to build the work halfway up the Capuchin road, where the terrain was "not very rocky, with only very small differences in elevation" which otherwise would have involved a "minor addition to the cost of excavation." Moreover, the commission leaned toward a structure of "separate cottages [...] capable each one of twenty or thirty beds. It is evident that the solutions proposed were very cautious, connected to the doubt about the effective capacity of attracting the neighboring population on the part of the hospital once it is made operational, as well as about the availability of sufficient funds for the construction and successive handling of a more important complex." Feeling sorry, Padre Pio confided to Francesco Lotti[65]: "These gentlemen want to build the hospital where it must not be." And he charged him: "Listen, do me a favor: leave this very night and go to Pescara. There you will go to the study of engineer Candelori: ask his address from the Abresch who know him. Ask the engineer, in my name, to give you that hospital project, made some time ago, by a designer of his, which he should have kept. You must do in such a way as to return before tomorrow afternoon, when there will be the last gathering of the Commission." The person delegated accomplished the mission in time and when the friar showed it to the Commission, he said: "I thank you for all the trouble you have assumed, but the hospital will be this and it will rise on the mountain, at the side of the convent" and everyone "literally remained speechless."[66]

The direction of the works was entrusted to Angelo Lupi of Pescara, who although he had neither degree nor diploma, in a short time transformed the farmers of San Giovanni Rotondo to specialized workers: electricians, woodworkers, carpenters, tile makers and mechanics.

By blasts of mines and by pickaxes "seventy five thousand cubic meters of rock" were excavated for the foundations. On

September 2, 1948 the first floor was laid, blessed by Padre Pio in the presence of Italian-American authorities.[67] On December 8, 1949 the last floor of the building was laid. It was now a matter of covering it inside and out and to set the technological fixtures.

On June 26, 1950 Doctor Sanguinetti, the delegate adviser of the Work, personally sculpted with hammer and chisel the name of the hospital at the top of the facade.

Alongside the site rose the first office for the handling of the correspondence and for the editing of the bulletin of the *Work of Padre Pio*.[68]

The entire landscape changed physiognomy. The bare mountain became covered with green thanks to the effort of reforestation realized by Sanguinetti "with more than one hundred thousand plants."[69]

On July 26, 1954, through an "intimate, silent and humble" ceremony, Padre Pio blessed and inaugurated the Health Center of the "Casa Sollievo della Sofferenza,"[70] made up of first aid and laboratory services of clinical analyses, general medicine, ear specialization, dentistry and paediatrics.[71] "Bear in mind that this is a work of charity," he said to the people present, "so it is necessary to serve it with the spirit of God." And he added: "The first thanksgiving goes to God for his work. He who has started will also end what he is designing with his hands."[72]

Among those present there was Doctor Franco Lotti, who at some later time, remembered:

> "'It will be a quiet inauguration,' said Sanguinetti. As soon as the inauguration ended, an hour after one had to begin. And we opened the outpatient clinics one hour after they were inaugurated and blessed by Padre Pio. 'This,' he said, 'is not an inauguration'

– also Sanguinetti wrote about it – 'it is a family ceremony so that the Padre may already see what has been realized. While the works for the construction of the hospital are being completed, the outpatient clinic must already start functioning.' And thus it was, practically. We quickly started working."[73]

The start of the sanitary activity posed the problem of the "juridical physiognomy" to be given to the future hospital. It was decided to establish a special Congregation of the Franciscan Third Order invoking and being under the patronage of Santa Maria delle Grazie, authorized with the consent of the diocesan archbishop on August 25, 1954 and by the Minister General of the Capuchins,[74] who entrusted to Padre Pio the task of spiritual director. This special Congregation, however, would handle the management of the Hospital only in 1957, after having obtained the juridical recognition on the part of the State and the authorization of the Pope[75] and after having stipulated a contract of lease for the real estate and the equipment with the Company Shares that, immediately after, assumed the denomination of "Immobiliare Casa Sollievo della Sofferenza."[76]

On November 5, 1954 the Blood Bank opened. The ceremony took place in an atmosphere of sadness because two months before, on September 6, Doctor Guglielmo Sanguinetti had died, and for him Padre Pio wept as for a brother.

His work as a delegate administrator first passed to Alberto Galletti[77] of Milan, then to engineer Luigi Ghisleri, also originally from the Lombard capital. The Milanese engineer, thanks to his acquaintances, made appeal to clinics of international fame, which promptly placed themselves at the disposition of Padre Pio, offering their services and to constitute the first staff of doctors, choosing them from among their students.

The first courses for male nurses also started and there were chosen as sisters to be destined to the department of hospitalization the Missionarie Zelatrici del Sacro Cuore di Gesù [Zealous Missionaries of the Sacred Heart of Jesus].[78]

In April 1955 the Lord granted eternal reward for his generosity to another pioneer of the Work: Mario Sanvico, who held the office of vice president of the Company Shares.[79]

Already in the first months of 1956 everything was ready for the inauguration of the Casa Sollievo della Sofferenza. Chosen for the date was May 5, name day of Padre Pio.

The Mass, presided over by the Founder was attended by a crowd of fifteen thousand persons, among whom were numerous religious, civil and military authorities. The Church was represented by the archbishop of Bologna, Cardinal Giacomo Lercaro, who gave a discourse marked by charity as a sign of the presence of God. But Padre Benigno da Sant'Ilario Milanese, Minister General of the Capuchin Friars, read also a telegram coming from the Holy See with the apostolic blessing of the Pope, Pius XII.

For the Italian State, present were the president of the Senate, Cesare Merzagora, and the minister of the Post and Telecommunications Office in the first Segni Government, Giovanni Braschi.

After the intervention of Cardinal Lercaro, Padre Pio gave a memorable discourse in which he traced the guidelines for his earthly work:

> "Gentlemen and Brothers in Christ, the Casa Sollievo della Sofferenza is finished. I thank the benefactors from all parts of the world who have given their cooperation. This the creature Providence, helped by you, has created; I present it to you. Admire it and bless together with me the Lord God.

A seed has been planted on the earth that He will warm with His rays of love. Do not deprive us of your help; collaborate in this apostolate of relief for human suffering."[80]

After the ritual cutting of the ribbon, done by Padre Pio and by Cardinal Lercaro, there was inaugurated a symposium of cardiosurgery at the world level regarding pathologies of the coronary arteries, presided over by Prof. Pietro Valdoni, with doctors coming from various countries of Europe and from the United States.[81] The following day the speakers went to greet Padre Pio who, with his natural simplicity, reminded them:

"You have the mission to cure the sick; but if at the bed of the sick you don't bring love, I don't believe that medicines are of much use. I have experienced this: my doctor – when in 1916-17 I was sick – my doctor, in treating me, brought me first of all a word of comfort. Love cannot do anything without the word. How could you express it if not through words that spiritually uplift the sick person? Then I went to a specialist who, unceremoniously said to me that I was a TB sufferer, and that I would have yes or no another year of life. I returned home with death in my heart, resigned to the will of God. And as you can see, I'm still here. The prophecy of the specialist has not taken place. But not all the sick people are like Padre Pio of 1916-17. Bring God to the sick; he will be of more value than any other remedy."[82]

The following May 8 the Congress participants were received in an audience by Pope Pius XII who described the Hospital of San Giovanni Rotondo as "the fruit of one of the highest intuitions, of an ideal that ripened after a long time and made perfect while contacting the most varied and cruel aspects of the moral and physical suffering of mankind."[83]

The hospital was furnished with three hundred bedspaces, but the heart of this whole complex was the chapel, built exactly at the center of the edifice, to be "the spiritual center that radiates its force toward all the other sections."

The first sick person was hospitalized five days after the inauguration. At the end of May the bedspaces occupied were barely 25.

"The Casa had as its disposal also a farm, at the foot of Mount Gargano, which supplied milk, eggs, poultry, oil and others. The grounds and the farmhouse had been donated to Padre Pio."

On the day of Corpus Christi, Padre Pio carried in procession the Blessed Sacrament to every part of the hospital. He returned at other times to visit the sick, for some baptisms, for processions, to assist at some prayers or to celebrate the Mass.[84]

After a short time the hospital began to be filled with the sick who came also from neighboring centers.

Starting on January 1, 1957 the Casa Sollievo della Sofferenza not only had all the bedspaces occupied, but it was rendered necessary to add supplementary beds in the rooms to meet the numerous requests. Padre Pio understood that it was indispensable to think of a widening, but also that it was necessary to give to the Work tranquillity and serenity from the juridical point of view. In March of that year, following the advice of Monsignor Giuseppe D'Ercole, teacher of Canon Law at the Pontifical Lateran University, who had studied the situation, he decided to write to the Pontiff[85] to propose to:

"a) entrust the management of the Casa Sollievo della Sofferenza to the Congregation of the Franciscan Third Order of Santa Maria delle Grazie of San Giovanni Rotondo (Foggia) which to that end will manage according to the norms proposed in letters b and c. (Such Congregation has been erected in an organic form by the Father General, with the consent of His Excellency, the Ordinary of Manfredonia, and has received recognition of its juridical personality from the President of the Italian Republic with a decree dated June 20, 1955);

b) to realize the management according to the purposes indicated by the undersigned to the pious wills of the donors and according to the mandate entrusted to him by the same wills, to be able to direct the aforesaid Congregation as Director (a task which the proponent already possesses, by decree of the Father General emitted on August 25, 1954) and, through Your Apostolic indult, to maintain such office of Director as long as natural life exists;

c) to carry out the tasks of the aforesaid management through the Work of the Tertiaries recruited among the members of the aforesaid Third Order, constituted in consultative committees (sanitary, cultural, administrative), remaining firm for the Third Order the statutory rules for the other activities that the same Third Order will carry out outside the Casa Sollievo, in conformity with the purposes declared by art. 2 of the Statutes;

d) to systematize the position of the real estate patrimony through the depositing of the shares at the Istituto delle Opere di Religione."

Moreover, Padre Pio asked the Pope that, after his death, "your Apostolic See accept as a donation the goods of the Work of the Casa Sollievo della Sofferenza and, possibly, destine them to the continuation of the Work itself."[86]

This letter was accompanied by an attachment, signed as always by Padre Pio, in which he repeated the request "to be able to deposit at the Istituto per le Opere di Religione, with consequent registration, the almost totality of the shares representing the real estate patrimony of the Società Casa Sollievo della Sofferenza." Also, he proposed "that the shares being talked about, be deposited to the credit of an account to be registered to Padre Pio da Pietrelcina for the Casa Sollievo della Sofferenza" and that he himself could "dispose of said deposit with all the rights and in his stead the Holy See will dispose of the same deposit." The document ended with the express intention of "leaving (with apposite and regular act of a last will) to the Holy See the values that he asks to be able to deposit and what other may be in deposit at the time of his death or on other entries, even posteriorly, regarding the account being talked about."[87]

On April 4, 1957 the assistant of the Secretariat of State, Monsignor Angelo Dell'Acqua, answered "that His Holiness, taking account of the importance of the hospital complex being talked about and of the nobility of the ends it looks at, has been kindly pleased to give You the favors You implore."[88]

Padre Pio named as his procurator the same Monsignor D'Ercole, who kept the task for six months. At the expiration of the mandate the Founder chose Angelo Battisti, a spiritual son of his who was an employee in the Secretariat of State of the Holy See as the sole administrator of the "Real Estate" Society. However, Doctor Kisvarday was chosen.[89]

On May 5, 1957, on the occasion of the first anniversary of the inauguration, Padre Pio gave a discourse in which he traced prophetically the development of his Work on earth, hoping that it might become "a temple of prayer and science, where the human race may find itself in Jesus Crucified as a single sheepfold, with one shepherd" and where "patients, doctors, priests will be reserves of love, which the more will be abundant in one, the more it will communicate itself to others." And he added:

"Starting today, let us resume the second stage of the journey to be accomplished. The journey to be done is this: the Work still recommends itself to your generosity so that it may become a hospital city technically prepared for the most daring clinical requirements. The Casa must increase the number of beds."[90]

This, therefore, was his will, in spite of the debts still to be paid, also because the three hundred had soon become insufficient.

On May 5, 1958, the excavation of the mountain resumed under the direction of Angelo Lupi, called by Battisti. On July 16 Padre Pio blessed the first stone of the new wing, poured on the digging a spoonful of concrete and signed the memorial parchment which, sealed in a leaden tube and enriched with so many other signatures, was buried beside the first stone. Once more Providence proved the friar right. The Work was gradually brought to completion until August of 1966, guaranteeing the doubling of the bedspaces.[91]

Meanwhile, the future was also considered. On October 14, 1960, based on the paper work exchanged with the Holy See in the first months of 1957, Padre Pio signed a testament, then modified on May 11, 1964, to nominate the "Holy See, and through it, the Supreme Pontiff pro-tempore, universal heir of all goods, movable and immovable, belonging to me, at any rate entitled to me [...] for example, the Work of Padre Pio da Pietrelcina, the Casa Sollievo della Sofferenza."[92]

On May 5, 1966 the first ten years of the life of the Clinic were celebrated. At the Mass, presided over by Cardinal Lercaro, Padre Pio, already prostrate due to age and illness, had to assist seated in the midst of his confreres and spiritual children. For the occasion a message of his was disseminated in which he blessed "all those who in whatever way have cooperated in the birth and development of the Work" and which contained a particular thought "for the Prayer Groups, already spread throughout the world and present here today, on the occasion of the ten years of the 'Casa', for their second International Convention. At the side of the Casa del Sollievo, they are in the frontline positions of this City of Charity, are breeding grounds of faith, hotbeds of love, wherein Christ himself is present each time they gather for prayer and the Eucharistic Agape, under the guidance of their Pastors and spiritual Directors." Then he added:

> "It is prayer [...] that moves the world, that renews consciences, that supports the 'Casa,' that comforts the suffering, that heals the sick, that sanctifies work, that lifts up sanitary assistance, that gives moral force and Christian resignation to human suffering, that spreads the smile and blessing of God on every languor and weakness."[93]

Two years after, on September 23, 1968, Padre Pio ended his earthly pilgrimage. But before dying he succeeded to have approved the project of a new, large wing of the hospital to bring the bedspaces from 600 to 848. The works began on July 6, 1969, and ended on the first of June 1973, with the inauguration and the blessing imparted by Cardinal Mario Nasalli Rocca of Corneliano, whom a few days before Pope Paul VI had named as "Patron of the Work of Padre Pio."

This inauguration had been preceded by notable changes. The Holy See nominated as administrator both of the "Real Estate" Society and for the management of the clinic Professor Raffaele Politi who continued to get the help of Angelo Battisti, as his delegate, for the coordination of the activities in the place.

Hence, by decree dated April 14, 1970, the Secretariat of State of the Vatican set up the "Foundation of Religion and of Cult the 'Casa Sollievo della Sofferenza' – Work of Padre Pio of Pietrelcina," civilly recognized on January 14, 1971 by decree of the President of the Republic. Designated as first president was Monsignor Oreste Vighetti, of the Secretariat of State.[94]

Further expansions began in 1978, after the arrival of the new president, Monsignor Riccardo Ruotolo. Among these, the two most important have been: the opening of the complex of the residence for the elderly: "Casa Padre Pio" on the Capuchin road, a few hundred meters from the clinic, that took place on May 25, 1987,[95] and the realization of the fourth outpatient clinic,[96] dedicated to "John Paul II," inaugurated on June 1, 2002.[97] In this structure located on Padre Pio driveway, at about 500 meters from the hospital, is carried out the greater part of the outpatient clinic services. The departments of paediatrics and of paediatric oncohematology have been placed in environs furnished to make less oppressive the hospitalization of children. Two entire levels of the outpatient clinic, moreover, have been destined for research, with modern and advanced scientific laboratories, used by personnel of proven professionalism, which has allowed achieving important results in the sector of genetics.

The commitment of study, in reality, was started in 1991 and underwent an important development in September of 1997, when Prof. Luigi Gedda gave to the "Casa Sollievo della Sofferenza" the Istituto Mendel, with seat in Rome which, from that moment on, has partnered with and integrated the work being carried out in San Giovanni Rotondo with about thirty scientific projects.[98] Thanks to this notable activity, on July 16, 1991 the Minister of Health and that of the University and Scientific Research have attributed to the "Casa Sollievo della

Sofferenza" the title of Istituto di Ricovero e Cura e Carattere Scientifico [Institute of Recovery and Care of a Scientific Nature], allowing the Work of Padre Pio to realize studies in the "field of genetics, immunology and various diseases that strike also because of hereditary-family causes."[99]

The last goal was reached on September 13, 2015, with the inauguration of the Institute of Regenerative Medicine, built alongside the outpatient clinic and blessed by the Secretary of State of Pope Francis, Cardinal Pietro Parolin, with as goal the "production of human stem cells […] for experimentations and therapies on patients" and the "study of genomics and of molecular mechanisms" in the field of oncology.[100]

Thus, the prophetic plan traced by the Padre founder has come to full realization. "A Center of Intercontinental Studies," he said on May 5, 1957, "must assist the doctors in perfecting their professional culture and their Christian formation."[101]

The Center of Professional Formation

The site of the "Casa Sollievo della Sofferenza" and, starting 1954, also that of the new conventual church, brought serenity to so many families reduced to misery by the Second World War. However, they were not enough to reduce in a significant way the high rate of unemployment, particularly high in the whole of Southern Italy, including San Giovanni Rotondo. The phenomenon was particularly evident in the area of the convent:

> "Adults and young people crowded the flight of steps and the waiting room, sometimes even the corridors of the convent. There was established a new contact with the poverty of the fathers of

families (the female members of the Third Order Franciscans, notwithstanding their precious action of greater outreach, clearly could not arrive everywhere) favoring unemployed or underemployed young men."[102]

This depressing phenomenon did not pass unobserved in the eyes of Padre Pio who, on the first occasion, turned to the Guardian, Padre Carmelo da Sessano del Molise, and asked him: "Young man, tell me something: all these young men, what do they come here to do? We never saw them before! What is happening?" "Padre," the superior answered, "these young men, these poor people, are unemployed; they don't find work. They would like to work, but unfortunately!" "And so?" asked the stigmatized Capuchin with a little "malicious" smile. Padre Carmelo chose to remain silent, having understood that the answer he had in mind and was about to give was not the one he wanted to hear. But that silence could not last long. "And so," the Guardian found the courage to admit, "they come here to ask for alms and I give them, to one 500 lire, to another 300…" All in all, it was a work of charity. But that smile of Padre Pio gave to Padre Carmelo the strong sensation of having said something that was not quite right. And, effectively, he did not even succeed in finishing his answer. The person he was talking to opened wide his eyes and almost shouted: "What! Young men twenty years old asking for alms! And when will they begin to work to earn their bread? Alms at twenty years of age! So that their poor parents, who should be aided by them, find themselves in the situation of having to provide food for their twenty-year-old children! They should work! They should work!" "They have good will," Padre Carmelo said, trying to justify them, "but there are no jobs." But Padre Pio did not want to listen to excuses and suggested with a tone that made it appear that the suggestion was almost a command: "Teach them an art or a trade! They must work to earn their bread! Go to Rome to our friends and do something."[103]

Between the two there was a pact, made known after the death of the charismatic friar by his already ex-Guardian:

> "On the evening of my arrival in San Giovanni Rotondo, on October 10, 1953, as superior of the convent, I had a confidential talk with him, which is the keystone of our interpersonal rapports. […] That evening I clearly said to him that I had gone, although reluctantly, not as "his superior," but as his "spiritual son" and also that I remained such in that condition, so that I besought him to tell me always what pleased and what displeased him.
>
> He accepted this, my proposal, with evident difficulty and with unease, and in fact on several occasions, I had to remind him of the pact."[104]

Thus, that desire of Padre Pio became an order for Padre Carmelo who, without waiting for new proddings, "went in search of an Entity that dedicated itself to the qualification of young men and 'unearthed' Emilio Bevilacqua, owner of the hotel S. Maria delle Grazie, who knew Atty. Giuseppe Bersani, a practicing Catholic and brother of engineer Saverio, director in Rome of INAPLI, Istituto Nazionale Addestramento Professionale Lavoratori Italiani [the National Vocational Training Institute of Italian Workers]." Through the latter, the Guardian of the Capuchins of San Giovanni Rotondo succeeded in having his request reach the table of the President of the Institute, Marcello Valentini, who showed himself favorable to the proposal, but laid down a condition, explaining that "the direction of the center, INAPLI, could not be entrusted to a friar." When Padre Pio learned about this, his answer was clear-cut: "Not even in our dreams should we accept this Entity." In fact, he not only "wanted some religious to direct the works in favor of young men," but he also desired that the center be "religious and Franciscan at the same time [...] because it was necessary to form men not only with human values, but also with those spiritual and Christian ones."

Padre Carmelo, therefore, turned to the "Ente Meridionale di Cultura Popolare [Southern institution of Popular Culture], whose president the honorable Michele Troisi was very happy to start with his own equipment the activity of the Center headed by a religious." Moreover, he went to Rome, together with the Provincial Minister Padre Agostino da San Marco in Lamis, to meet the General Procurator of the "Istituto dei Terziari Cappuccini dell'Addolorata [Institue of Tertiary Capuchins of the Sorrowful Mother],"[105] who "dedicated himself to the technical instruction of the youth under the guidance of Padre Urbano Lapuente." The two "examined the Constitutions and concluded that they had found the solution for San Giovanni Rotondo," not only for the professional formation of young men, but also for "the Parish of Sant'Onofrio, located in the periphery of the town, near the cemetery," which was provisionally entrusted to the pastoral care of the Capuchins. Thus "the archbishop of the Diocese of Manfredonia, Monsignor Andrea Cesarano, accepted that the new friars would create, in the area of the district of Sant'Onofrio, the Center of Professional Formation and would also take care of the parish."

On the first of November 1957 Padre Domenico Serini arrived. He, 16 days after, took possession of the parish and, at the same time, worked at the side of Padre Carmelo in the activities of founding the center of professional formation. In the beginning he did not even have autonomous lodging and lived provisionally in the convent of the Capuchin Friars Minor. Successively "three locales were rented out from private persons" in which were held the first courses for welders and repair mechanics. With the arrival of two other tertiary Capuchins of the Addolorata, Padre Giovanni Caravaggio and Padre Francesco Galante, the first community was formed and, finally, on January 27, 1958, there was the official inauguration of the Center dedicated to Saint Joseph the artisan, that seven months after, at the end of the first courses, was visited by the Minister of Labor, Luigi Gui.

Soon were added other courses for ulterior professional qualifications: building carpenters, blacksmiths, printers and the provisional locales became insufficient. Padre Carmelo and Padre Domenico "had known that a dear friend of the friar with the stigmata, Tonino Lecce, possessed a wide piece of land in the zone, so-called 'Travaglio' who was willing to cede and, thanks also to the good offices of another […] friend, Nicola Fini," it was acquired "for a symbolic price." Taking care of the project was engineer Saverio Bersani and, thanks to other helps of Providence, which allowed the finding of the necessary funds, "in barely three years, the construction was realized and the transfer took place in a gradual way, occupying now one wing, now another," although the finishing touches were only done in 1965. In the meantime, some young men trained in San Giovanni Rotondo, after having been "examined by a Commission of German labor," had obtained a "labor contract […] in Germany," while others were employed in the factories "of some industrialists in North Italy, who came […] as pilgrims to Padre Pio."

Each year new courses were added and, in the first twenty-five years, "a good 3,454 students obtained professional qualification" in 17 training fields.[106] After having overcome, in the middle of the 1970's, "a critical situation, above all due to the difficulties coming from the Region of Puglia," a few years later "the evolution of society and the legislative innovations as regards Professional Formation" induced "the Center of Training to constitute itself as ITCA/FAP (Istituto Terziari Cappuccini dell'Addolorata/Formazione Aggiornamento Professionale [The Institue of Tertiary Capuchins of the Addolorata for Up-to-date ProfessionalTraining]), but the "change in name" has not affected "overmuch the elements of crisis," as it has not affected the reconstitution of ITCA/FAP as Onlus, which took place in April of 1998. Only by reducing the formative activity and renting out, starting in 2002, part of the locales to the Istituto Tecnico Commerciale Statale, did the Center succeed in finding economic equilibrium guaranteeing its own survival."[107]

When he was still living, Padre Pio periodically received those young men who were preparing themselves to become qualified laborers, to whom he recommended: "Young men, remember that before becoming good workers, it is necessary to become good Christians."[108]

The Kindergartens

When Padre Carmelo arrived in San Giovanni Rotondo in 1953, the zone called 'Santa Croce' was then experiencing a notable increase in housing even in the midst of general indifference. As is always the case everywhere, those who suffered the most from such a situation were the weak and the children. For the latter there was just one kindergarten run by the Suore Adoratrici del Sangue di Cristo (Sister Adorers of the Blood of Christ), "located in the upper part of town which proved to be completely unsatisfactory as regards location, structure and functionality with respect to the requirements of a growing town."

To a worried Padre Guardian who "lacked experience because up to that moment he had never been interested in social problems and still less 'in mathematics' Padre Pio suggested that it was necessary to move in order to resolve the various problems." These difficulties were also compensated for through the help of Nina Campanile who "long ago had known Mother Eleonora Foresti, foundress of the Istituto delle Suore Francescane Adoratrici, an Institute that Padre Pio had inspired and of which he was, with the Mother, author of the Rules of the emerging Order." The teacher from San Giovanni Rotondo, therefore, had the idea of inviting these Sisters "to direct the first kindergarten, in the zone of Santa Croce." And so Padre Carmelo "gave into the pressing demands, above all of those of his friars, not to mention those of Nina Campanile […] in spite of the many doubts that assailed him." These were destined to dissolve by recognizing in all of this "the work of the Lord, the supreme inspirer of everything and at the same time the supreme solver of every problem."

Having obtained the permission of the Archbishop, Monsignor Andrea Cesarano, there was the problem "of finding a building […] to use as a mother house and no matter how hard they looked for it, it was never found." Only "in the spring of 1955 were they able to purchase a piece of land situated in the 'Santa Croce' area and great was the joy of all, but especially of Padre Pio, who offered to the Lord his ongoing bodily sufferings." The needed money was placed at the disposal of the convent and "in the face of urgent social needs and at the holy insistence of Padre Pio, no one opposed the acquisition." It was only the first step. The time required to build the structure seemed too long. Meanwhile, "the residents of the neighborhood of 'Santa Croce' continued to increase almost exponentially, while the children who had urgent need of intervention had become about two hundred." Padre Carmelo's awareness, at this point, faced a choice: the path of legality and that of charity. He chose the latter and "decided to replace the building still under construction, with a 'lighter' structure to be used at least temporarily as a kindergarten … even though it was unlawful." So, in this surrogate building, the first Kindergarten called 'Santa Maria delle Grazie', without "any State and Municipal authorities' permission and even without any Sisters," was opened. In order to take care of the first 132 pupils the Franciscan Third Order under Mrs. Filomena whom the Padre did not hesitate to call 'dynamic and indefatigable' took charge. Meanwhile, the executor of the will of the holy Capuchin friar was beginning "to receive help and subsidies left and right. [...] Only in the second half of 1956 did the authorization for the operating status of the school by the Provveditorato agli Studi di Foggia [Authority for Education in Foggia] arrive and almost simultaneously came news of the imminent arrival of the Sisters," while the building destined for the Kindergarten was still under construction.[109]

While the first illegal Kindergarten was up and functioning, there appeared a still more complex problem in another part of town: in the area of Sant'Onofrio where "the Protestants had constructed a place of worship and a kindergarten for children," to whom they taught "hatred for the Church and, especially, out of Satanic instigation, against the Madonna," telling them that "the saints are blocks of wood" and that "the Most Holy Virgin had many children." Because of this, one day, turning to Padre Carmelo, Padre Pio said to him: "Have you heard about what is happening in the town and particularly in the district of Sant'Onofrio?" The Guardian "answered that he did not know anything also because that zone […] was under the pastoral jurisdiction of the mother church." But when he came to realize the situation personally "he went to the bishop of the Diocese, Andrea Cesarano, to seek the authorizations to start a Catholic social work that envisioned not only a second kindergarten but also the professional formation of young women in the area of tailoring and sewing."

Here, too, the activity was begun in the town by the "Third Order Franciscans in a provisional way," while the direction was entrusted "provisionally," in expectation of a definitive solution, "to a Franciscan Sister adorer, whose Institute already operated in the Santa Croce area." It was November 7, 1956. At the same time he obtained news of the availability upon their arrival from Sicily of a group of "Capuchin Sisters of the Sacred Heart, who were open to the social, educational and didactic activities of infants and young girls." Padre Pio would convince the Mother General when she came to San Giovanni Rotondo to "take a quarter of the Sisters from each of their places," explaining that "it is God's will that you open this House." After the arrival of the Sisters on December 8th of that year, there was a "private" ceremony to commemorate the beginning of their kindergarten apostolate dedicated to "St. Francis of Assisi," while the public dedication took place on December 17th, the same day that the kindergarten dedicated to "Santa Maria delle Grazie" was inaugurated. On both occasions the great Inspirer of the two works and Archbishop Cesarano were present. During the return trip in the Fiat 1100 that had driven them, Padre

Pio, still dazed by that great feast, said to Padre Carmelo: "But what have you done!…". And while he said these words, "he laughed with satisfaction and joy.…"

"The opening of the new kindergarten marked the end of the activities of the other religions in the area of Sant'Onofrio and in fact already in the first few days a great many, even of different faiths, enrolled their children in the new kindergarten" and "in the space of a few months the Protestants were forced to close their asylum definitively" to open it in another area of town. Soon the "provisional seat" showed itself unable to cope with the "continuous enrollments to the new kindergarten" which "reached and surpassed two hundred, while the available spaces were much less." Trusting in Divine Providence, on January 16, 1957, the Superior General of the Capuchins of the Sacred Heart, Sister Aurelia di Maria Ausiliatrice, signed a contract for the acquisition of the residence of the Giuva family which was located in the neighborhood of the church of Sant'Onofrio, "having more than 4 thousand square meters of frontage." It "was renovated in lightning speed" and, in "less than two months, it was modified […] to house the sisters and the little orphan girls on the first floor," since the religious, soon after their arrival on December 8, had opened an orphanage for a number of abandoned children and the moral salvation of many abandoned and helpless waifs."[110] Instead, the ground floor was made fit to host "the nursery school, chapel, parlor and various other services." On February 4, moreover, a work room named "Saint Clare," in which "the young women of the area were instructed in the arts and crafts of dressmaking, sewing and embroidery," was inaugurated and, on the same day, it was "named and blessed after that Franciscan Sister Adorer of the Holy Cross, Saint Veronica Giuliani."[111]

The Protestants, after having closed their asylum in the area of Sant'Onofrio, reopened it "in the last zone that remained free and available, in the 'Case nuove' district west of the town." Having taken note of his unique ability, Padre Pio and Archbishop Cesarano once more turned to "Padre Carmelo for the establishment of a third Franciscan kindergarten." The Guardian, in June of 1957, went to Pietradefusi, in the Province of Benevento, to meet the Suore Francescane Immacolatine [the Franciscan Immaculatine Sisters] who "accepted the proposal with enthusiasm and declared themselves honored to be invited to San Giovanni Rotondo," but, as usual, "financial difficulties appeared." Also this time, there was hope "in the help of Divine Providence." Within a few days, under pressure from his holy confrere, Padre Carmelo, together with the vicar and Bursar of the Friary, Padre Raffaele da Sant'Elia a Pianisi, met with the owner of the land, agreed on a price and, soon after, put together a project "in record time." The contract was signed by the "Mother General of the Suore Immacolatine" and the convent paid an advance of "a certain sum." The remainder, to be paid in two semestral instalments, was paid by the Institute of the Sisters. Yet one more time, while waiting for the construction of the building, the "urgent need" induced them "to lease some places that were more or less sufficient and suitable," where the Sisters could live and where the activities of the kindergarten and of a "dress-making and sewing room" could be initiated. "On November 7, 1957 the first Franciscan Immaculatine Sisters arrived, led by the Mother General," and were received by Padre Pio, who exhorted them "to do ever more and better, at the service of the Lord and of the Immaculate Virgin." Two months later, on the same day the Center for professional training, also the kindergarten "Pace e bene" along with the adjoining workroom were inaugurated and blessed. The "new areas" were completed in 1959.[112]

The "San Francesco" Consumer Cooperative

The Sant'Onofrio district was founded by brick-makers from the Sangiovannesi district known as "Stalingrad" because many of the inhabitants of that district were enrolled in the Communist Party which, in that area, had also "founded a flourishing consumer cooperative which offered merchandise at very low prices," so much so that it was frequented by "many Catholics."[113]

There was always a risk that these could be "infected" by materialistic and anti-religious Marxist ideology. And this wasn't just a hunch:

"Radio Prague advocated struggle and victory with constant propaganda reminders using the slogan: 'We must win San Giovanni Rotondo, where there is the so called Holy friar at all costs.'"[114]

That's why Padre Pio urged Padre Carmelo to: "Create our own Guild."

Once again the Guardian of the convent obeyed his "subject" and, with the help of "a group of Padre Pio's spiritual children," in June of 1955 a Cooperative of Catholic Consumers, which took off the ground in a very short time, was born:

"In less than two years the Cooperative showed itself to be a thriving business with a budget of a few million lire which at that time seemed a lot. With that income it was possible to distribute, in the name of Padre Pio who remains the living image of Christian charity, an extraordinary number of goods to alleviate the misery of many needy people."[115]

Notes on Chapter IV

1. Cf. "Letters of Padre Pio to Padre Benedetto of March 26, 1914," P. da Pietrelcina, *Epistolario*, M. da Pobladura, A. da Ripabottoni (Ed.), Edizioni Padre Pio da Pietrelcina, San Giovanni Rotondo (FG) 1995, vol. I, pp. 462-463.

2. Anonymous, "The 'miracles' of a Capuchin in S. Giovanni Rotondo," in *Il Giornale d'Italia*, year XIX, n. 123, May 9, 1919, fourth edition.

3. Argo, "The 'Saint' of S. Giovanni Rotondo,"in *il Foglietto*, year XXII, n. 20, May 25, 1919.

4. The slip of the writer, who obviously was not of the place, is evident as he confused Foggia with San Giovanni Rotondo.

5. Translation by F. Tuohy, "The friar of Foggia," in *Daily Mail*, June 19, 1920, p. 4.

6. Cf. F. Castelli, *Padre Pio e il Sant'Uffizio (1918-1939). Fatti, protagonisti, documenti inediti*, Edizioni Studium, Rome 2011, p. 67.

7. "Letter of Padre Pio to Padre Benedetto of June 14, 1920," in *Epistolario*, op. cit., vol. I, pp. 1170-1171.

8. "Letter of Padre Benedetto to Padre Pio of June 1920," in *Epistolario*, op. cit., vol. I, p. 1172.

9. M. Capuano, "Precedents of relief of suffering in San Giovanni Rotondo," in *La Casa Sollievo della Sofferenza*, year XV, n. 5, March 1-15, 1964, p. 4.

10. Cf. ibid.

11. F. Morcaldi, *San Giovanni Rotondo nella luce del francescanesimo*, Tipografia Grafiche Gitto, Foggia 2004, p. 20.

12. Cf. A. Fabrocini, "Report to the Council of Adminstration of the Congregation of Charity of San Giovanni Rotondo," April 9, 1922, in *Positio super virtutibus*, op. cit., vol. III/1, pp. 464 and 465. "*La Monte*, also called *Monte frumentario Cavaniglia*, had been instituted in the year 1679 by the duke *don Geronimo Cavaniglia e dalla Università di San Giovanni Rotondo* and had the task of helping the farmers – citizens needing through loans quantities of grain, even free of charge" (S.A. Grifa, *I luoghi della memoria di San Giovanni Rotondo – Storia e Toponomastica*, Edizioni Gargaros, San Giovanni Rotondo (FG) 2011, p. 94). The Monte frumentario, with its less than praiseworthy offshoots, ceased to exist in 1876" (Ibid, p. 95).

13. "Resolution n. 140," in *Registro delle deliberazioni della Congregazione di Carità (September 20, 1914 – April 19, 1926),* in *Historical Archives of the Municipality of San Giovanni Rotondo.*

14. Cf. "Resolution n. 154, Report of the meeting of the Congregation of Charity," October 29, 1922, in ASCSGR.

15. "Report of the Commission for the Civil Hospital," January 3, 1923, in ASCSGR, Category 2, Class 2, File 1, Folder n. 14 (1924-1925).

16. "Resolution n. 273," in *Registro delle deliberazioni della Congregazione di Carità,* in ASCSGR. Cf. also G.G. Siena, *Padre Pio e S. Giovanni Rotondo nei disegni della Provvidenza,* Bastogi, Foggia 2002, pp. 141-142.

17. "Resolution n. 317," in *Registro delle deliberazioni della Congregazione di Carità,* in ASCSGR.

18. Cf. *Positio super virtutibus,* op. cit., vol. III/1, p. 466.

19. Cf. F. Morcaldi, *San Giovanni Rotondo alla luce del francescanesimo,* op. cit., p. 21.

20. Dated February 8, 1929, the Congregation of Charity "deliberates who is to be nominated as director of this Hospital in place of the bereaved Doctor Francescantonio Giuva, and chose Doctor Merla Angelo Maria fu Matteo" and "in place of Doctor Merla Angelo Maria promoted to be Director the nominated Vice Director of this Hospital, Mr. Morcaldi Tommaso fu Antonio," both "for two years, from last January, to December" 1930, except confirmed according to law" ("Resolution n. 151 and 152," in *Registro delle deliberazioni della Congregazione di Carità,* in ASCSGR).

21. Cf. ibid.

22. Founded by the Servant of God Clelia Merloni.

23. Founded by Saint Maria de Mattias.

24. Cf. *Positio super virtutibus,* op. cit., vol. III/1, p. 467.

25. Draft of the letter of the Mayor Bramante to the President of the Congregation of Charity, November 7, 1931, in ASCSGR n. 476.

26. Draft of the letter of the Mayor Bramante to Mr. Centra Michele di Antonio, November 9, 1931, in ASCSGR, n. 9932.

27. Answer to the note of the president of the Congregation of Charity to the Mayor, prot. n. 104, November 22, 1931, in ASCSGR, Category 2, Class 2, File 1, Folder n. 14 (1924-1925).

28. Letter of the Prefect of Foggia to the Mayor of San Giovanni Rotondo, November 28, 1931, doc. 2/2 n. 35814, in ASCSGR, Category 2, Class 2, File 1, Folder n. 14 (1924-1925).

29. Draft of the letter of Mayor Bramante to S.E. the Prefect of Foggia, November 12, 1931, in ASCSGR, n. 9902.

30. Answer to the note of the President of the Congregation of Charity to the Mayor and Municipal Councilors of San Giovanni Rotondo, prot. n. 1046, December 8, 1925, fg. 2, in ASCSGR, Category 2, Class 2, File 1, Folder. 14 (1924-1925).

31. G.G. Siena, *Padre Pio e S. Giovanni Rotondo nei disegni della Provvidenza*, cit, p. 145.

32. Ibid, p. 147.

33. Data of the Istituto Nazionale di Geofisica e Vulcanologia (www.ingv.it).

34. According to *La Gazzetta del Mezzogiorno* (year XV, July 1937, p. 2) in San Severo the earthquake of July 17 caused damage and wounds, of which two are serious, while "in the nearby Municipalities the tremor has been barely felt, and light damages with cracks in the buildings have been verified only in San Paolo di Civitate and in Serracapriola, and along the railways of San Severo-Termoli."

35. R. da Sant'Elia a Pianisi, "Hints about the most relevant episodes regarding the life of Padre Pio of Pietrelcina," in CP, vol. XXX, p. 2390.

36. Cf. ibid.

37. It's about a part of the area where the "Casa Sollievo della Sofferenza" now stands.

38. Cf. R. da Sant'Elia a Pianisi, "Hints about the most relevant episodes regarding the life of Padre Pio of Pietrelcina," in CP, vol. XXX, p. 2390; *Positio super virtutibus*, vol. III/1, p. 468.

39. "Diary of Mario Sanvico," in G. Leone, *Padre Pio e la sua Opera*, op. cit., pp. 41 and ff.

40. Cf. F. Chiocci, L. Cirri, *Padre Pio. Storia di una vittima*, op. cit., vol. II, p. 21. A *leaflet* of the 1950's reports almost completely the words said by Padre Pio that evening: "Evils are the children of the guilty, of the betrayal that man has perpetrated against God… But God's mercy is great… a single act of love of man towards God has so much value in his eyes that He would consider it as a small thing to repay it through the gift of all creation… Love is none other than the spark of God in men… the essence itself of God personified in the Holy Spirit… We, poor creatures, should dedicate to God all the Love of which we are capable… Our love, to be adequate to God, ought to be infinite, but unfortunately, only God is infinite… However, we must employ all our energies in love, such that the Lord one day may say to us: 'I was thirsty

and you gave me to drink; I was hungry and you gave me to eat; I suffered and you have consoled me…'. The man who, surpassing himself, bends over the wounds of his unfortunate brother lifts to the Lord the most beautiful and noble prayer, born of sacrifice, of love lived and realized, of dedication in body and in spirit… In every sick man, there is Jesus who suffers! In every poor person, there is Jesus who languishes! In every poor sick person there is Jesus who suffers and languishes twice!" (G. Leone, *Padre Pio e la sua Opera*, op. cit., p. 48).

41. Cf. ibid, p. 44.
42. Cf. ibid.
43. Cf. ibid, p. 38.
44. It is the title of an article, unsigned, that appeared in *La Gazzetta del Mezzogiorno* on January 13, 1940, on p. 5, in which it is reported that "for three days it is raining without interruption."
45. On the topic, see also: Anonymous, "The collapse of the railroad bridge over the Carapelle river," in *La Gazzetta del Mezzogiorno*, January 19, 1940, p. 3; Anonymous, "The bad weather in Capitanata," in ibid, January 25, 1940, p. 5; Anonymous, "The floods in Capitanata," in ibid, January 26, 1940, p. 3; Anonymous, "The floods in Capitanata," in ibid, January 27, 1940, p. 5; Anonymous, "For the floods in the various Zones of the Tavoliere," in ibid, February 7, 1940, p. 5.
46. Taken from the Register of the Resolutions of the Mayor of San Giovanni Rotondo, Resolution n. 87 of September 2, 1944 having as object: "Urgent repairs for the real estate owned by the Municipality destined for the civil Hospital – Transfer of funds," in Archives of the State of Foggia, Prefecture, The payment, the series, and the envelop 84, file 2.43.19, fg. 1.
47. Cf. "Resolution n. 123" of August 24, 1940, in *Registro delle Deliberazioni del Podestà dal 15-6-1940 al 23-4-1942*, pp. 57 and ff.
48. Before Italy's entrance into the war, the sum had already been collected of "a million and a half" lire which, "to avoid a depreciation of the money was invested in the acquisition of a piece of land in Lucera," in the province of Foggia (Cf. G. Leone, *Padre Pio e la sua Opera*, op. cit., p. 45).
49. Cf. *Positio super virtutibus*, op. cit., vol. III/1, pp. 471 and ff.
50. They were: "Doctor Guglielmo Sanguinetti, Doctor Carlo Kisvarday, the priest Father Giuseppe Orlando, the lady Doctor Engineer Eleonora Figna, Doctor Guglielmo Panicali, Mr. Pasquale De Meis […],

and Doctor Sanvico. And then Angela Serritelli, one of the first followers of Padre Pio; Count John Telfener, Mario Cacciaglia of Sulmona; the Marquis Giambattista Sacchetti, a long time friend of Padre Pio […]. Then there were the Marquis Bernardo Patrizi, the lawyer Daniele Ungaro, the lawyer Giovanni Pennelli and others" (G. Leone, *Padre Pio e la sua Opera*, op. cit., p. 51).

51. Cf. ibid, p. 49.
52. Cf. ibid, p. 51; *Positio super virtutibus*, op. cit., vol. III/1, p. 473.
53. Cf. G. Orlando, *"Profeta. Storia della chiesa e del convento di Pietrelcina,"* ds, p. 49.
54. Ibid, p. 58.
55. Cf. G. Leone, *Padre Pio e la sua Opera*, op. cit., p. 48.
56. Acronym of *United Nations Relief and Rehabilitation Administration* (Amministrazione delle Nazioni Unite per l'assistenza e la riabilitazione). It is an international humanitarian organization founded by the ONU in 1943 for the economic and civil assistance of peoples affected by the Second World War.
57. Cf. *Positio super virtutibus*, op. cit., vol. III/1, p. 475.
58. Born on December 11, 1882 in New York, he died in the same city, of which he had been mayor, on September 20, 1947.He was the son of Achille La Guardia, a musician who emigrated from his native Cerignola (in the province of Foggia) and of Irene Coen Luzzatto, an Italian Jew native of Trieste.
59. Cf. G. Leone, *Padre Pio e la sua Opera*, op. cit., p. 56.
60. Regarding this, only hypotheses have been formulated but not supported by any documentation.
61. Cf. S. Luzzatto, *Padre Pio. Miracoli e politica nell'Italia del Novecento*, Einaudi, Torino 2007, p. 304.
62. Cf. ibid, p. 307.
63. Cf. "Memorial of Sirio Giametta (first part)," in P. Scarano, "Padre Pio said to me: 'Build me a hospital,'" in *Gente*, year XLI, n. 13, April 1, 1997, pp. 87 and ff.
64. Cf. "Memorial of Sirio Giametta (second part)," in P. Scarano, "The Friar guided my hand in building the hospital," in *Gente*, year XLI, n. 14, April 8, 1997, p. 57.
65. The future chief Pediatrician of Casa Sollievo della Sofferenza.
66. F. Lotti, *Padre Pio nella mia vita, quando lo straordinario era quotidiano*, Luciano Lotti (Ed.), Edizioni Padre Pio da Pietrelcina, San Gio-

vanni Rotondo (FG) 2015, pp. 96 and ff. A reliable source, but it cites neither documents nor testimonies, sustains that the project "was signed by engineer Candeloro," but "it came out that a man called Angelo Lupi had done it. He was neither an engineer nor a surveyor. But his design was convincing; it lent itself to the nature of the place. Thus it was chosen, and he himself was called to direct the works" (G. Leone, *Padre Pio e la sua Opera*, op. cit., p. 69).

67. In the same year "an Italian-American worker sent to the Casa some dollars, requesting to destine them to the poor sick. The administrators were very much moved by that offering, then they thought: "What if we set up a fund purposely for those who don't have money?" The fund was established and to it was given the name of the Italian-American worker who was the first to think about the poor sick: Mario Gambino fund. The worker was very happy when he learned about this and he sent other dollars, and his ten children sent other dollars" (Anonymous, "The Gambino fund," in *La Casa Sollievo della Sofferenza*, year IV, n. 12, June 16-30, 1953, pp. 1-2).

68. Cf. G. Leone, *Padre Pio e la sua Opera*, op. cit., pp. 69 and ff.

69. Cf. ibid, p. 88.

70. Cf. Giesse, "Family feast," in *La Casa Sollievo della Sofferenza*, year V, n. 15-16, August 1-31, 1954, p. 2.

71. Cf. G. Leone, *Padre Pio e la sua Opera*, op. cit., p. 95.

72. D. Serini, *Padre Pio e le opere sociali*, Edizioni Pugliesi "Eremo Santa Maria delle Grazie," Acquaviva delle Fonti (BA) 2004, p. 93.

73. Interview to Professor Francesco Lotti, given to the author on April 29, 2006.

74. Cf. G. Leone, *Padre Pio e la sua Opera*, op. cit., pp. 95 and ff.

75. Cf. *infra*.

76. Cf. *Positio super virtutibus*, op. cit., vol. III/1, pp. 494 and ff.

77. The task of Galletti lasted barely three months because of disagreements with Lupi and with the other directors of the Work. Even his successor had disagreements with Lupi, but he resolved them by dismissing him and substituting him in the direction of the works with engineer Giannangeli of Pescara (Cf. G. Leone, *Padre Pio e la sua Opera*, op. cit., pp. 102-103).

78. Cf. ibid, pp. 100 and ff.; Ibid, p. 116.

79. Cf. Anonymous, "Mario Sanvico has passed away," in *La Casa Sollievo della Sofferenza*, year VI, n. 9, May 1-15, 1955, p. 2.

80. G. Leone, *Padre Pio e la sua Opera*, op. cit., p. 108. "These also spoke: the Marquis Sacchetti, Engineer Ghisleri, the Mayor of San Giovanni Rotondo Francesco Morcaldi, Professor Nylin, president of the European Society of Cardiology and finally Doctor Giovanni Gigliozzi" (Ibid).

81. Cf. ibid, p. 111.

82. Ibid.

83. Cf. ibid, pp. 112-113.

84. Cf. ibid, p. 116; Ibid, p. 120 and p. 143.

85. Cf. ibid, p. 126.

86. F. Chiocci, L. Cirri, *Padre Pio. Storia di una vittima*, op. cit., vol. III, pp. 255-256.

87. Ibid, p. 257.

88. Ibid, pp. 258 and ff.

89. Cf. G. Leone, *Padre Pio e la sua Opera*, op. cit., p. 132.

90. Ibid, pp. 127-128.

91. Cf. ibid, pp. 132 and ff. The last department of the first extension, that of otolaryngology, was opened on August 1, 1966, after the arrival of the designated consultant, Prof. Graziano Pretto, coming from the University of Padua and student of Prof. Michele Arslan (the news was given directly by Prof. Pretto to the author during a talk on August 13, 2015).

92. "Version of 1964," in G. Pagnossin, *Il calvario di Padre Pio*, Tipografia Maffeo Suman, Conselve (PD) 1978, vol. II, p. 217. For a deepening of the question, Cf. S. Campanella, *Obœdientia et pax. La vera storia di una falsa persecuzione*, op. cit., pp. 162 and ff.

93. G. Leone, *Padre Pio e la sua Opera*, op. cit., p. 167.

94. Cf. ibid, pp. 203 and ff. Cf. also O. Vighetti, "The Holy Spirit powerfully works here," in *La Casa Sollievo della Sofferenza*, year XXIV, n. 12-13-14, June 16-July 31, 1973, pp. 42-43.

95. Cf. ibid, p. 275. The blessing was imparted by the Cardinal Secretary of State Agostino Casaroli.

96. The second was opened on January 22, 1964 and substituted for the one started ten years before (Cf. G. Leone, *Padre Pio e la sua Opera*, op. cit., p. 161), while the third was blessed by Cardinal Casaroli.

97. The blessing was imparted by the Apostolic Nuncio in Italy, Monsignor Paolo Romeo (Cf. Anonymous, "The outpatient clinic 'John Paul II' inaugurated", op. cit., in *Voce di Padre Pio*, year XXXIII, n. 9, September 2002, pp. 40-41).

98. Cf. M. Fontana, "From a donation by Luigi Gedda a new impulse for genetic research," in *La Casa Sollievo della Sofferenza*, year LII, n. 9, May 1-15, 2001, pp. 11-12 (article taken from *L'Osservatore Romano* of January 21, 2001).

99. Cf. R. Ruotolo, "1992: first year of the Institute of biomedical research," in *La Casa Sollievo della Sofferenza*, year XLIII, n. 1, January 1-15, 1992, p. 4.

100. Cf. Anonymous, "The Institute of Regenerative Medicine," in *La Casa Sollievo della Sofferenza*, year LXVI, July-August 2015, pp. 6-7. The article specifies that to the stem cells "one arrives by using the epidermal or blood cells of the patient, that is, the adult cells that are transformed into cells of the embryonic type, without however producing embryos and thus overcoming the problems of an ethical nature. Such reprogrammed cells do not contain any extraneous genetic viral material, maintaining at the same time all the genetic information of the single patient." A few weeks before the inauguration of the Institute of Regenerative Medicine, the scientific director of "Casa Sollievo della Sofferenza," Professor Angelo Vescovi, has announced that on June 5, 2015 "brain stem cells have been transplanted in his cervical spinal marrow, for the eighteenth and last patient affected by Amiotrophic Lateral Sclerosis (sla) within a clinical experimentation of Phase I authorized by the Superior Institute of Health in 2011," announcing the "preparation of an experimental protocol of phase II […] for the purpose of evaluating the betterment of the dosage of the cells and their potential therapeutic efficacy." The first phase, in fact, has served to "evaluate the evolution of the disease after the treatment and the security and the harmlessness of the same" (Cf. A. Vescovi, "Stems: end of the experimentation of phase I with brain stem cells in SLA," in ibid, pp. 8-9).

101. Cf. G. Leone, *Padre Pio e la sua Opera*, op. cit., p. 127.

102. A. da Ripabottoni, *San Pio da Pietrelcina. Cireneo di tutti*, Edizioni Padre Pio da Pietrelcina, San Giovanni Rotondo (FG) 2011, p. 492.

103. Cf. ibid, p. 493.

104. D. Serini, *Padre Pio e le opere sociali*, op. cit., p. 95.

105. Founded "in Spain by a Capuchin bishop, Mons. Luigi Amigò y Ferrer, for the purpose of rehabilitating wayward and marginalized young men, through professional formation and in light of modern pedagogy and psychology" (Ibid, p. 149).

106. Cf. ibid, pp.150 and ff.
107. Cf. A. Impagliatelli, D. Scaramuzzi, *La periferia si è fatta centro. I cinquant'anni dell'ITCA*, Sao ko kelle terre Editrice, San Giovanni Rotondo (FG) 2008, pp. 106 and ff.
108. D. Serini, *Padre Pio e le opere sociali*, op. cit., p. 15.
109. Cf. ibid, pp. 107 and ff.
110. "The Spiritual Padre," Padre Carmelo will remember, "could not hold back his tears, when the first group of orphaned children gathered in the shadow of Saint Anthony of Padua, to whom was dedicated the new orphanage, were presented to him." (Ibid, pp. 128-129).
111. Cf. ibid, pp. 115 and ff.
112. Cf. ibid, pp. 133 and ff.
113. Cf. ibid, p. 81.
114. A. da Ripabottoni, *San Pio da Pietrelcina. Cireneo di tutti*, op. cit., p. 494.
115. D. Serini. *Padre Pio e le opere sociali*, op. cit., p. 81.

AFTERWORD

Upon reaching the end of reading this, once more one cannot but remain amazed confronted with the figure and the action of Saint Pio of Pietrelcina as an instrument of the mercy of God.

As Benedict XVI called to mind during the *Angelus* of Sunday March 30, 2008:

> "Mercy is in truth the central nucleus of the gospel message; it is the name itself of God, the face with which He has revealed himself in the Old Testament and fully in Jesus Christ, the incarnation of creating and redeeming Love. This merciful love illumines even the face of the Church, and it is manifested both by means of the Sacraments, in particular that of Reconciliation, and by the works of charity, whether communitarian or individual. All that the Church says and does manifests the mercy that God nourishes for man."

Undeniable and surprising, in this Capuchin priest, is the tireless being at the disposition of those – and we know that they were so many and their number was constantly increasing – who asked mercy and forgiveness from God. Equally undeniable and surprising is the manner with which the saint of Gargano with the stigmata "moved" throughout the whole world, without ever leaving San Giovanni Rotondo, to "move" sinners to search for the merciful God.

His "rough" action – some episodes show this with extreme clarity – his being "gruff," already seen by many and in many ways, was not but the method used by him to call back the sinner, so as to situate man in his creatureliness, to make the Christian aware of how much the love of God, manifested, made present and reachable in Jesus Christ, was the most precious pearl and the greatest of all gifts.

His "going" in search of man needful of grace, with that extraordinary and unique phenomenon given to him of bilocation, was always and only a sign of the love of the merciful God, first in love, first in searching, first in waiting for, as a beggar, man's answer of love. Saint Pio of Pietrelcina reveals here an extraordinary aspect of the Gospel: he is a servant who works in the vineyard of the Lord, so that nothing may be lost and all of us may have the necessary preoccupation to produce fruit that is good, abundant, fragrant and sweet.

Side by side with this work of spiritual mercy, also undeniable in Saint Pio of Pietrelcina is his concrete action in the works of corporal mercy in the intuition, foundation, construction and development of the hospital "Casa Sollievo della Sofferenza." The Christian touched by grace cannot but feel the pain of humanity which searches for the meaning of its own suffering and true happiness. The man marked with the wounds of Love had to feel the suffering and voices of those who are sick and in need of care.

Saint Pio of Pietrelcina knows that the spiritual man, if he does not want to betray his union with God, is called to concreteness, to a laborious action, to not close his eyes in front of one touched by the mystery of pain and sickness. A mystery that has no answers if not in a judgment founded on faith in Jesus Christ, the Crucified One who lives! The mercy of God in the sacrament of Reconciliation is the clearest expression of the forgiveness without reserve of the Lord, which surpasses all measure. The "God rich in mercy" (Eph 2:4) who in Jesus "became flesh" (Jn 1:14) reveals the redeeming Love that gives itself continually and without pause, infinitely, for those who recognize Him.

Saint Pio, however, knows and is aware how mercy and forgiveness are difficult to accept by a man who is full of himself, stubborn in wanting to be like God, unhappy when his creatureliness and dependence on another person are being contested.

The only way to call to and attract to mercy and Love, says Saint Pio of Pietrelcina, proposed by the Holy Father Francis as an icon of this Jubilee of Mercy, is to restore to God the gift received, recognizing that all good things come from the Lord, without keeping anything for ourselves, giving of ourselves without reserve in the service of Love.

Saint Pio, secluded in his convent, seated in his confessional, active in the material and spiritual construction of the "Casa Sollievo della Sofferenza," has not done anything except restore what has been received from the Lord: participation in the sacrificial offering of Jesus, the Son, and he has done it well aware that he had to struggle first of all against himself, so as not to fall under the illusion that he, Padre Pio, is the one who is dispensing the mercy, the forgiveness, the charity and the help.

The assaults of the demon, the beatings, the injuries, the false accusations, have not been anything except trials on the part of God, to maintain the union of that servant of His with Him, as Christ on the cross.

The mercy of God, through the proclamation of the Jubilee, still one more time is placed at the center of the Gospel announcement, and Saint Pio of Pietrelcina is – even today – an announcer of this mercy through his peculiar mission, one that is unique, exceptional, personal and unrepeatable. If we could – but it is possible only in the communion of saints – meet the eyes of Saint Pio of Pietrelcina, we would see two eyes that shine with charity and direct ours to Christ, the living icon of the mercy of the Father.

Pope Francis, proposing Saint Pio of Pietrelcina as an icon of the mercy of God, does nothing except put back in first place in the announcement of the Gospel, God, His Love for mankind, His forgiveness which has no limits, His Church, the place where the mercy of God is sacramentally dispensed and where people learn to serve the suffering members of humanity and those who with sincerity go in search of their destiny.

Fra Carlo Calloni, OFMCap.
General Postulator